THE SCRIPT READER'S CHEAT SHEET

WRITE FASTER COVERAGE
BECOME A BETTER SCREENWRITER

LEE HAMILTON

THE SCRIPT READER'S CHEAT SHEET
Write Faster Coverage - Become a Better Screenwriter

First Edition
Copyright © 2022 by Lee Hamilton

All rights reserved. Neither this book nor any portion thereof may be reproduced or used in any manner whatsoever without the express written permission of the publisher, except for the use of brief quotations in a review. Inquiries should be addressed to: scriptreaderscheatsheet@gmail.com

ISBN 978-1-7391398-0-3

www.scriptreaderscheatsheet.com

To Frank
Never stop being awesome.

CONTENTS

INTRODUCTION 10
HOW TO USE THIS BOOK 17
COVERAGE TIPS 19
LAYOUT 23
LOGLINE 27
SYNOPSIS 29
PREMISE 30
    TITLE 31
        THE TITLE IS MISLEADING 31
        THE TITLE COULD CAUSE OFFENCE 32
    GENRE 33
        GENRE IS UNCLEAR 33
        IT DOESN'T ADD ANYTHING NEW TO THE GENRE 34
        THERE AREN'T ENOUGH GENRE CONVENTIONS 35
    THEME 36
        THE OVERALL THEME OR MESSAGE IS UNCLEAR 37
        THERE ARE TOO MANY THEMES 38
        THEME ISN'T REFLECTED IN THE SUBPLOTS 39
        THE THEME DOESN'T GET RESOLVED 39
    TONE 40
        THE TONE ISN'T IMMEDIATELY CLEAR 41
        TONE ISN'T STRONG ENOUGH 42
        TONE IS INCONSISTENT 43
    ORIGINALITY 44
        IT'S TOO SIMILAR TO ALREADY PRODUCED MATERIAL 44
        IT'S SO UNCONVENTIONAL, IT'S CONFUSING 45
        THE STORY IS BASED ON THE WRITERS BORING LIFE 46
        THE STORY IS A BORING FACT-BASED ADAPTATION 47
    MEDIUM 49
        IT DOESN'T FIT THE CHOSEN FORMAT 49
        THE CONCEPT DOESN'T HAVE LEGS 51
    LENGTH 52
        THE SCRIPT IS TOO LONG OR TOO SHORT 52
        POOR FORMATTING HAS ALTERED THE PAGE COUNT 53
        ALTERING THE PAGE COUNT WILL ADD DESIRABILITY 54
    MARKETABILITY 55
        IT ONLY HAS NICHE APPEAL 56
        IT WON'T APPEAL TO ITS TARGET AUDIENCE 56

IT'S TRYING TO PLEASE TOO MANY PEOPLE	57
IT LACKS INTERNATIONAL APPEAL	58
THERE'S A LACK OF DIVERSITY	60
BELIEVABILITY	61
CHARACTERS MAKE IMPLAUSIBLE DECISIONS	61
THERE ARE NOTICEABLE PLOT HOLES	63
BUDGET	64
THERE ARE TOO MANY CHARACTERS	65
THERE ARE TOO MANY LOCATIONS	66
THE WRITER SITES COPYRIGHTED MATERIAL	67

STRUCTURE 69

OPENING SEQUENCES	70
THERE'S NO HOOK	70
THE MC ISN'T IN THE FIRST SCENE	71
THERE'S TOO MUCH SETUP	72
SETUPS & PAYOFFS	73
SETUPS AREN'T PAID OFF	73
PAYOFFS AREN'T SETUP PROPERLY	75
SETUPS ARE TOO OBVIOUS	75
STORY BEATS	76
THE PREMISE IS UNCLEAR DURING THE FIRST ACT	77
TURNING POINTS AREN'T CLEAR ON THE PAGE	78
THERE'S A WEAK POINT OF NO RETURN	79
THE END HOOK IS WEAK	80
SCENE STRUCTURE	81
THE PLOT HASN'T ADVANCED BY THE END OF THE SCENE	82
SCENES REPEAT NEEDLESS INFORMATION	83
SCENES HAVE NO CONFLICT	84
SCENES ARE TOO LONG	85
SUBPLOTS	87
THERE'S A DISTINCT LACK OF SUBPLOTS	87
THERE ARE TOO MANY SUBPLOTS	88
SUBPLOTS AREN'T LINKED TO THE CENTRAL STORY	89
SUBPLOTS DON'T MERGE DURING THE FINAL ACT	90
NARRATIVE DEVICES	91
FLASHBACKS ARE USED UNNECESSARILY	92
MONTAGES DON'T ADVANCE THE PLOT	93
INFO IS REVEALED IN THE WRONG ORDER	94
THE READER HASN'T UTILIZED THE 'RULE OF THREE'	95

CHARACTER 97

CHARACTER INTRODUCTIONS	97
PHYSICAL APPEARANCES ARE TOO DETAILED	98
VITAL INFORMATION IS MISSING	99
ACTION ISN'T REVEALING CHARACTER	100

- GENDER ISN'T IMMEDIATELY CLEAR ... 100
- CHARACTER NAMES ARE CONFUSING ... 101
- MAJOR CHARACTERS HAVEN'T BEEN NAMED ... 102
- CHARACTERS ARE NUMBERED INSTEAD OF NAMED ... 103
- GOALS ... 104
  - THE MC HAS NO CLEAR GOAL ... 104
  - THE MC'S GOAL ISN'T INTERESTING ENOUGH ... 105
  - THE MC'S MOTIVATIONS ARE UNCLEAR ... 106
- FLAWS, WEAKNESSES, AND LIMITATIONS ... 107
  - THE MC IS TOO PERFECT ... 108
  - THE MAJOR FLAW ISN'T TIED TO THE CENTRAL PLOT ... 109
  - THE MC'S WEAKNESS DOESN'T BECOME A STRENGTH ... 110
- STAKES ... 111
  - THERE ARE NO CLEAR STAKES ... 111
  - THE STAKES AREN'T BIG ENOUGH ... 113
  - THE STAKES DON'T INCREASE THROUGHOUT ... 114
- ROOT-ABILITY ... 115
  - THE MC IS TOO UNLIKABLE ... 115
  - CHARACTERS ARE ONE-DIMENSIONAL ... 117
  - THE CAST LACKS DIVERSITY ... 118
  - IT'S UNCLEAR WHOSE STORY IT IS ... 119
  - CHARACTERS AREN'T EMOTIONALLY ENGAGING ... 120
- CHARACTER ARC ... 121
  - THE MC HASN'T CHANGED BY THE END OF THE STORY ... 121
  - CHARACTER ARCS AREN'T BELIEVABLE ... 123
  - THE MC DOESN'T HAVE ENOUGH ACTOR BAIT ... 124
- ANTAGONISTIC FORCE ... 124
  - THERE IS NO ANTAGONISTIC CHARACTER ... 125
  - THE ANTAGONIST ISN'T DEVELOPED ENOUGH ... 126
  - THE ANTAGONIST LACKS ENOUGH SCREEN TIME ... 127
  - THE ANTAGONIST IS A WEAK RIVAL ... 128
- SUPPORTING CHARACTERS ... 129
  - SECONDARY CHARACTERS OVERSHADOW THE MC ... 129
  - SECONDARY CHARACTERS HAVE MORE SCREEN TIME THAN THE MC ... 131
  - SECONDARY CHARACTERS DON'T SERVE ANY REAL PURPOSE ... 132
  - SECONDARY CHARACTERS ARE ONE-DIMENSIONAL ... 133
- PASSIVE CHARACTERS ... 134
  - THE MC ISN'T SOLVING THEIR OWN PROBLEMS ... 134
  - THE MC DOESN'T DRIVE CHANGE ... 135

DIALOGUE ... **137**

- EXPOSITION ... 138
  - THERE'S TOO MUCH DIALOGUE ... 138
  - DIALOGUE IS TOO ON-THE-NOSE ... 139
  - THERE'S TOO MUCH FILLER DIALOGUE ... 140

THERE'S TOO MUCH Q&A DIALOGUE	141
DIALOGUE REPEATS INFORMATION WE ALREADY KNOW	143
WORDING IS REPETITIVE	144
THERE'S TOO MUCH TECHNICAL JARGON	145
VOICE	146
CHARACTERS SOUND TOO ALIKE	147
DIALECTS AND ACCENTS ARE OVERUSED	148
DIALOGUE ISN'T REALISTIC	149

PACE 151

DRAMATIC MOMENTUM	151
THERE ARE NOTICEABLE LULLS IN THE STORY	152
THERE ARE NO 'CATCH YOUR BREATH' MOMENTS	153
REPETITION OF INFO HAMPERS THE PACE OF STORY	154
THERE'S A LACK OF WHITE SPACE ON THE PAGE	155

READABILITY 157

TITLE PAGE	157
THERE IS NO TITLE PAGE	158
CONTACT DETAILS ARE MISSING	158
THE TITLE PAGE HAS UNNECESSARY ELEMENTS	159
FORMATTING	160
STANDARD INDUSTRY LAYOUT IS INCORRECT	160
THERE ARE TOO MANY FORMATTING ERRORS	162
SCENE HEADINGS ARE CONFUSING	163
PARENTHETICALS	163
PARENTHETICALS ARE USED UNNECESSARILY	164
PARENTHETICALS ARE USED TOO OFTEN	165
PRESENTATION	166
THERE ARE HUGE PARAGRAPHS OF TEXT	166
THE SCRIPT HASN'T BEEN PROOFREAD	167
SCENE HEADINGS ARE TOO LONG	168
BOLD OR CAPS HAVE BEEN OVERUSED	169
EXPOSITION IS CONFUSING	170
CHARACTER NAMES ARE INCONSISTENT	171
THERE ARE 'UNFILMABLES'	172
THE SCRIPT NEEDS MORE POLISH	174
SCENE DESCRIPTION	175
WRITING IS NOVELISTIC	175
GENRE ISN'T REFLECTED IN THE TONE	177
ORPHANS NEED TO BE CUT	178
SENTENCE STRUCTURE IS POOR	178
DIALOGUE IS WRITTEN IN THE SCENE DESCRIPTION	179
THERE'S TOO MUCH SCENE DESCRIPTION	180
SCENE DESCRIPTION REPEATS INFORMATION	181
VITAL INFO IS MISSING OR IN THE WRONG ORDER	183

ACTORS ARE BEING OVER DIRECTED	*184*
THERE'S TOO MUCH DETAIL	*185*
OVER DIRECTING	186
THERE ARE TOO MANY CAMERA DIRECTIONS	*187*
THERE ARE UNNECESSARY SHOT TRANSITIONS	*188*
VISUALS	189
THE WRITER IS TELLING, NOT SHOWING	*189*
THE CONCLUSION	**192**
VERDICT	**194**
WHAT NOW?	**195**
INDEX	**197**
THE CHEAT SHEET CHECKLIST	**199**

INTRODUCTION

If you want to break into screenwriting, there are few jobs more helpful to kick off your career than becoming a script reader. Reading screenplays isn't just a reader a great way to find work in the industry, it's one of the single best ways to improve your own writing. While script reading can be a rewarding career on its own, the role is often viewed as a stepping-stone job because good readers with creative ability can quickly advance through the ranks to become development execs, literary agents, showrunners, and filmmakers. Others who discover working in development is their calling can advance into positions such as script editor, storyliner, consultant, producer, Head of Development, or perhaps achieve the ultimate goal; to become a paid screenwriter.

Whether you're already employed as a reader, want to break into the industry, or are simply a screenwriter looking for effective ways to improve your craft, this is the book for you.

WHAT DOES A SCRIPT READER ACTUALLY DO?

Well, read screenplays, obviously, but why, for who, and to what purpose?

I'm betting that if you're reading this book, you're also an aspiring screenwriter. You're not alone. There are thousands, if not hundreds of thousands of people all over the world putting virtual pen to paper, sharing the same dream of having their brilliant screenplay produced into a movie, TV-show, short film, web series, fiction podcast, or whatever medium they're writing in. Finishing a screenplay is but the first hurdle in that process, the next is finding someone who is actually going to read it.

Script readers work in a myriad of positions alongside writers at various stages of their writing careers. Some are there at the beginning of a writer's journey, helping them to hone the craft, offering advice on how to improve stories, and ensuring that scripts are industry-ready. Some are judging scripts submitted into contests, assessing screenplays of all levels with an eye to help new talent break in, boosting the contest in the process. And some will be there to filter through the hundreds of submissions made to agents, managers, and studios, trying to capitalize on a compelling concept or harness a promising writer to add to their roster.

The script reader is the first in a series of gatekeepers that a writer must pass as they attempt to break in. Producers, production companies, agents, directors, actors, and studios all employ readers to assess the thousands of scripts that they wouldn't otherwise have the time to read. Readers evaluate which scripts have the potential to sell/buy and which writers have the potential for further work. They have the power to stop a script in its tracks, but they also have the ability to elevate a script to a higher level, to champion it, and to help take it to the next stage.

There are basically three different types of readers; contest readers, coverage readers, and studio readers. There are plenty of other film industry roles that involve reading screenplays as part of the job, but these three are the careers most accessible to new screenwriters. The essence of the role is mostly the same in each, but with slight variations. Contest and coverage reading often go hand in hand as screenwriting contests who also operate coverage services will look for readers who can do both, but it's not impossible to have a career solely doing one or the other.

CONTEST READERS

This is an entry-level position and a great place to start when trying to get your foot in the door. There are tons of great screenwriting contests out there, such as **The Academy Nicholl Fellowship**, the **Austin Screenwriting Contest**, **ScreenCraft**, **Slamdance**, **Bluecat**, and **Shore Scripts** to name but a few. All hope to discover hot new talent, and each of them receive thousands of contest submissions every year, and guess what? All of those entries need to be read and assessed before each deadline is met. It's a mammoth task that requires plenty of hungry readers. Here's the lowdown:

- Work remotely. As long as you've got an internet connection, you can do this from anywhere in the world.
- Salary ranges from an average of $3-$15 per read. The pay is usually lower during the early rounds, but this can increase closer to the final stages of a contest.
- You usually only need to read up to 40-pages during the early stages of a contest where it's easier to sift out the poorer scripts from the better ones, but as the contest advances, you will be expected to read scripts in their entirety.
- Work freelance. This isn't a payroll position, so you can be dropped as quickly as you were picked up. It's not uncommon for readers to work for several contests to ensure that they have a year-round income.

- Some contests require a minimum amount of scripts to be read, others allow you to pick up as many reads as you want, while others may require you to claim reads on a platform such as **Coverfly**. This means that if you don't get in there quick enough, another reader on the roster could jump in and grab any scripts going before you can, making it a first-come-first-serve job.
- Writing coverage can be an optional bonus. If a contest offers additional coverage to a writer (usually for a higher entry fee), there's every chance that you'll have the ability to do these too.
- You'll have to score each script and provide the rationale to support your decision. You may be asked to write a logline to prove that you've read enough of the script too.
- There's no interaction with the scriptwriter unless a contest offers additional coverage questions to be answered via coverage.
- You may need to provide a coverage sample to the company when applying to show that you're aware of the screenwriting basics or have a resume that reassures you don't need any training.
- There are limited networking opportunities, but it's a good start to your screenwriting resume.

COVERAGE READERS

Rather than simply judging the quality of a screenplay, as you would do when reading contest submissions, readers who also write coverage need to use their analytical skills to relay their thoughts on what works, what doesn't work, and why, back to the writer. This comes in the form of a coverage report. Here's the lowdown:

- Work remotely. As long as you've got an internet connection, you can do this from anywhere in the world.
- Average salary ranges from $25-115. This depends on the length and quality of the feedback. If you're an independent script reader who isn't working for a coverage service, you can charge whatever you like, but be aware, it can take a long time to establish a good reputation, especially if you don't have the relevant experience.
- You must read the entire screenplay.
- Work freelance. The pros are that you can work whenever you want and take on as much work as you want. The cons are that work can be inconsistent, so working for two or more companies is useful.

- You'll have to submit previously written coverage samples or write coverage on a script given to you by the coverage service in order for them to assess your abilities. You don't get paid for doing this.
- You need to have an excellent understanding of screenplay structure, formulating story, character development, what makes a script marketable, screenplay formatting, and all the other elements that come into play when trying to write and sell a script.
- Your notes go directly back to the writer, so you need to have great communication skills, be able to back up your reasoning using specifics from the script whenever possible, and be constructive but not demeaning.
- There are limited networking opportunities, but this is a great stepping-stone job in the industry.

STUDIO READERS

This is the coveted position for anyone who wants to break into Hollywood because of the excellent networking opportunities and hands-on experience available. That makes it the most competitive of the three roles to get, especially for those not living in L.A. It's also the better-paid position (eventually), but it also requires a high work ethic and exceptional drive in anyone vying for this role. Here's the lowdown:

- Ideally, you need to work on location. There's a whole host of admin duties and in-person tasks that go alongside this job, so you really need to live wherever the job is situated.
- Working as an intern first, which is usually unpaid, is the most common way to get your foot in the door. Most interns are graduates, but don't let that put you off if this doesn't apply to you. Bump up your resume with as much screenwriting and filmmaking experience as you can instead.
- If you're kept on after being an intern, you'll be on the payroll, which gives a little more security and a little less anxiety than working freelance.
- You must read the entire screenplay.
- You'll be writing coverage for studio executives rather than the screenwriter, but you'll need to be able to justify your assessment just as much.

- You need to have an excellent understanding of screenplay structure, formulating story, character development, what makes a script marketable, screenplay formatting, and all the other elements that come into play when trying to write and sell a script.
- There will be a higher amount of scripts to read at a faster turnover rate, so learn to read quickly if you can.
- Reading scripts and providing coverage is just one element of this role. You may also be required to answer phone calls, reply to emails, fetch lunch, liaise with agents & managers, and do other general office work.
- It's a great way to network and meet other industry professionals, creating the opportunity to move into development or production much faster than the other two reader roles mentioned previously.

It's possible to earn a living by doing all of these different reader jobs, but more often than not, it's a starting point from which to grow professionally. Good readers invariably move on to bigger things and this high turnover means that new positions regularly need filled. If you can demonstrate that you know the basics of screenwriting, becoming a reader could be your first step too.

WHY BECOME A READER?

The obvious reason is that if you're trying to become a great screenwriter, you're going to need to read tons of screenplays anyway, so why not get paid for it, right? That's a simplistic way of looking at it, but there's a lot of truth to this statement too.

One of the most frequent recommendations that a reader will make is that the writer should read more scripts, as it's very clear when a writer has neglected this aspect when learning the craft. Poor formatting, over-description, novelistic writing, unrealistic dialogue, and the inability to write compellingly are all key giveaways. Many new writers don't realize that their script needs to be as enjoyable to read as it will be to watch simply because they haven't put themselves in the position of being the *reader*, rather than the writer.

As a reader, you quickly begin to recognize the patterns and inconsistencies that make a read boring, eye-rolling, or unnecessarily difficult, and once you can see it in other people's writing, you'll start to notice when it's happening in your own work too. Having to provide your rationale to other writers on why certain aspects of their script aren't working and giving advice on possible improvements will allow you to look at your own writing with much more objectivity than you previously could.

The flip side is that you also get to learn from writers who are doing it right. When you read a script that's got captivating description written with a unique voice, intriguing characters who are active throughout, clever use of subtext, expertly crafted setups and payoffs, and dramatic momentum that makes you want to keep turning the page, it gives you the opportunity to figure out exactly how that's being achieved and you can subsequently apply that to help improve your own writing.

> "I have limited writing time as it is. Why would I waste time reading other people's scripts?"

That's a bit like a musician saying that they're only going to spend time composing their own music because they don't have time to listen to any other artists out there. Sure, it can be done, but why limit the amount of knowledge, understanding, and inspiration you could be exposed to in the industry in which you want to excel? I'm sometimes astounded why aspiring writers become determined to make things harder for themselves when it's already hard enough to break in.

Reading and analyzing screenplays isn't going to get in the way of you becoming a great writer, it's actually going to make you one more quickly. You become privy to all the reasons a script doesn't sell, why they don't win contests, or why they don't get produced. Being aware of what the person reading your script is looking for puts you at a distinct advantage above most other new writers out there.

In terms of kick-starting your career, a script reader is an entry-level job that can be an easy foot in the door to find. You can begin to build industry contacts, learn how the business works from the inside, and create an impressive resume should you want to become more involved in the development side. Almost everyone starts out wanting to produce their own material. The reality is the vast majority don't reach that pinnacle, but still find huge value and satisfaction working in the industry as collaborators on other people's projects. There's a huge assortment of industry roles that require the specialized skills that a script reader has to offer, making it an ideal stepping-stone job from which to frog-leap onto bigger things, or for those of us who are passionate about story, helping other writers develop, and using both the creative and analytical parts of the brain, it can be a rewarding career on its own.

KEY SKILLS NEEDED

You don't need a college degree to become a script reader, but having some formal training will certainly give you a head start. A film school diploma, a screenwriting qualification, or completing a script reader training course will all stand you in good stead when applying for positions, but for the complete newbie, there are plenty of free online resources, tutorials, and websites out there to help you gain just as much knowledge on the subject.

The key thing to do is practice. The more screenplays you read and the more script coverage you write, the more proficient you'll become. Recognized qualification or not, you'll still need to show examples of your work when applying for positions.

Coverage services, screenwriting contests, studios, agencies, etc., will all be looking for candidates that can demonstrate the following key skills:

- Must be familiar with industry-standard formatting.
- The ability to work quickly.
- Be up to date with current trends in film & TV.
- Understand the basics of what makes a good story and what constitutes as good writing.
- Be familiar with the various story structures used in film & TV.
- Have excellent communication skills and a critical eye.
- Dedication. Not every read is going to be an enjoyable one.
- A high level of objectivity.
- A love for movies and television.

HOW TO USE THIS BOOK

IF YOU'RE JUST STARTING OUT

For those completely new to script reading, take time to familiarize yourself with the basics by reading the LAYOUT, LOGLINE, and SYNOPSIS chapters. Go grab a screenplay you haven't read before, preferably a spec script (aka an unproduced script), and use it to practice with while reading this book. There are tons freely available online, but www.simplyscripts.com is a great place to get started.

Use the **Cheat Sheet Checklist** at the back of this book, or better still, download or print the fillable version from
https://www.scriptreaderscheatsheet.com/checklist
so that you have some idea of the elements you'll have to comment on.

Read your chosen screenplay. Taking notes along the way is a good way of speeding up the process, but find what works best for you. There are certain elements that can be commented on during the read, but some will require you to have read the entire script for them to be properly assessed.

Use the checklist while reading to cross off any potential problem areas so that you can come back to them later.

If you're including a synopsis, jot down what the major turning points and story beats are as well and what page they occur on as you encounter them for quick reference.

When you're ready, begin to write coverage. (Don't worry, there's a downloadable blank coverage template for you to use here:
https://www.scriptreaderscheatsheet.com/blankcoveragetemplate

As you come to each screenwriting element, refer to the corresponding subsection in this book to discover what you should look for, why it's helpful to highlight the issue to the writer, and to use any quick cheats that will help you write your report faster!

Adapt or alter the cheats to suit your own writing voice and build your own repertoire of repeatable phrases and advice to give.

IF YOU'RE A SEASONED READER

For those of you who, like me, are already screenplay-savvy, and have been writing coverage for a while, but want to speed up the process, feel free to skip the LAYOUT, LOGLINE, and SYNOPSIS sections. Use the **Cheat Sheet Checklist** at the back of this book, or better still, download or print the fillable version and use it to cross off any potential problem areas that you encounter when reading your next screenplay assignment:
https://www.scriptreaderscheatsheet.com/checklist

When writing coverage, use the cheat sheet as an instant reference to find the corresponding cheats and copy and paste them into your report during the read or after, whatever works best for you. Adapt any cheats to suit the material you are assessing or to better match your own personal delivery.

IF YOU'RE A SCREENWRITER

Use this book to better understand what exactly a script reader is looking for in a screenplay. You can do this by reading the whole book through, or better still, use it to self-assess your own work. Use the **Cheat Sheet Checklist** at the back of this book, or better still, download or print the fillable version from and use it as a guide during rewrites:
https://www.scriptreaderscheatsheet.com/checklist

Check off any element that your script could potentially receive a comment on and refer to each sub-chapter to discover what a reader is likely to advise and why. Keep doing this, making amendments in your screenplay along the way, until you feel your script is as polished and complete as it can be. Not only will this save you some valued money when it comes to purchasing coverage, it'll also help you determine the quality of the coverage you receive if you use a coverage service further down the line.

It's also advised that you do at least attempt to write coverage on a script that's preferably been written by someone else, whether that's a short, TV, or feature film. Once you look at other people's work with a critical eye, you'll begin to look at your own in the same manner too. It'll quickly become second nature to introduce effective elements while minimizing problematic ones in your own writing.

COVERAGE TIPS

There's an art to delivering coverage. You can't just give general statements or tell a writer you didn't like something (well, you can, but don't expect them to be a returning client). A writer took the time to put finger to keyboard and created something that they believe in. You've got to respect that, no matter what your personal opinion of the script is.

BE PRACTICAL

Reading an entire script and writing coverage can be time-consuming. Some readers will read a script once to get a first impression, then go back over it and pick talking points to expand on. Others will take notes when reading and refer to them when completing the report afterwards, while some might type up the coverage as they're reading the script. It's trial and error to begin with, so experiment and use whatever works best for you. Don't diminish the quality of your report, but try not to spend more time that it's financially worth on an assignment at the same time.

BE FORMAL

Unless you have a working relationship with a writer, write your feedback using a formal tone. This means referring to the writer (or better still, the writing) in the third person.

Use "the script", "the writing", and "the concept" instead of "your script", "you've", and "your idea", for example. Also avoid being overly personal by limiting uses of "I think", "I don't recommend", or "You".

You don't always have to be completely strict with this. Sometimes a personal comment, especially in the conclusion, can mean a lot to a writer, but in general, the emphasis should be on the writing and the story as much as possible.

JUSTIFY YOUR COMMENTS

It's important that you help the writer understand the reasons behind the advice or recommendations you're giving so that they can avoid making them again in future. There's no point telling a writer that something doesn't work if you don't explain why. That doesn't help anyone. Always try to put your comments into context by pulling an example from the script whenever possible, such as:

"Audiences may easily get lost in the long-winded discussions about targets, agencies, budgets, and resources, all of which often take place in an office or uninteresting location, risking the viewers tuning out while watching."

This helps a writer to better understand the case you're making. They don't have to take your advice, but at least they'll be able to argue their point against doing so.

BE OBJECTIVE

Unless working with an agent, studio, or a production company's particular remit, such as "We're currently looking for resonating LGBT stories" or "We want clear ideas that can deliver the highest quality popular mainstream drama to the largest audience.", you need to remain as objective about the material as possible. This means putting your own tastes and opinions to one side.

You have to be able to critique a piece of work regardless of whether you're a fan of that particular genre or if you find the subject taboo. Part of being a script reader is understanding where a script could fit amongst all genres, looking at the bigger picture, keeping up to date with current trends, and understanding the marketability of a project.

Be diplomatic. If a script is offensive, tone-deaf, or too risqué, it's not your job to correct someone else's worldview. You can, however, highlight how certain aspects of a script may hinder its marketability and general appeal. Keep the focus on the story. Does it work? Is it well-crafted? Is it sellable? Who will it appeal to? Is it original? Is it worth financing? Does the writer have talent?

BE POLITE

Remember that your report is supposed to help and encourage a writer, not criticize them to the point that they'll never want to write a screenplay ever again. We all have bad days, but try to remain professional. Don't be judgmental, snarky, or give personal opinions. Be approachable, understanding, and compassionate. Everyone starts off as a newbie writer. It's your job to guide them to the next level and beyond.

HIGHLIGHT THE POSITIVES TOO

Highlighting the elements that are also working in a script can be just as useful for writers to learn as opposed to only pointing out the elements that need work. This goes hand in hand with encouraging the writer. Offering praise on the stronger aspects of a script helps to round out a report and give balance. Some early screenwriters, especially one's perhaps purchasing coverage for the first time, are guilty of expecting a glowing report and they can be outraged when they don't receive one. Through practice, it shouldn't take too long to spot a veritable newbie writer, in which case, consider being more generous with highlighting the positive aspects of the script but without going overboard.

DON'T WASTE TIME REHASHING THE PLOT

If you're adding a synopsis to your report, there's no need to expand on this in the comment section. Unless you're using something as an example, re-telling the story becomes an obvious filler. It can be just as challenging to write a report on a well-crafted contest-winning screenplay with very little needing improved than with a script that's appalling on almost every level. You won't come across excellent scripts like this very often, but these are the reports that can leave you tearing your hair out as you try to figure out how to fill in the report page count. Regurgitating the plot and pulling out examples of what worked well and why can be a savior here, but a writer has paid to receive useful feedback, not for a re-telling of the story they already know, so do this sparingly.

THINK VISUALLY

There's a huge difference between how a story reads off the page to how it will look on screen, and a reader needs to keep this in mind. Initially, a script has to be good enough to 'get past the reader', meaning that more emphasis can often be placed on the readability over how the piece might translate visually, but also try to visualize the piece happening as you read too. This is a great way to catch any missing or illogical details in the scene description that might cause confusion. If a writer isn't thinking visually when writing, it'll quickly become apparent, as you'll also find it difficult to visualize the movie when reading the script.

UNDERSTAND THE BUSINESS

This should go without saying, but you also need to have a good general knowledge of what screenwriting is, what makes a great story, what makes great writing, and are up to date with current trends in the market. This means you've got to read a lot of screenplays, watch a ton of movies and television, and know what's hot and why.

Understanding act structure, what constitutes formulaic writing, how to identify original characters that resonate, and great dialogue is one thing, but you'll often be called upon to compare a concept with previously produced material, understand what particular audiences are looking for, and have a broad knowledge of genres and subgenres too. Learn to place a project within the context of the marketplace in order to fully assess its potential.

PROOFREAD

It has to be done, I'm afraid. There's nothing worse than pulling up a writer for having so many proofreading errors in their script that it hampered the read, but then being called out for having mistakes in your own report too. Pay particular attention to ensuring that you spell character names correctly in your feedback. If a writer gets the sense that you weren't paying attention when reading their script, you're increasing the chance of receiving a negative review or complaint.

LAYOUT

If you're working for a coverage service or a studio, you will be provided with that companies own individual template to use, but if you're starting up on your own, or are submitting sample coverage when applying for a reader position, here's a blank coverage template of what an average coverage report should look like: (**it's downloadable from the website too**)

COVERAGE REPORT

Title:	XXXXXX	Genre:	Drama, Sci-Fi, etc.
Writer(s):	XXXXXX	Circa:	Time Period
Pages:	XX Pages	Location:	Place/Setting
Format:	Feature/TV Pilot/Short etc.	Budget:	Low/Medium/High
Submitted by:	Your Name	Date:	XXXXXX

Logline: Sentence case……….

	EXCELLENT	GOOD	FAIR	POOR
PREMISE		X		
STORY		X		
CHARACTERS			X	
STRUCTURE			X	
DIALOGUE			X	
MARKETABILITY		X		

SYNOPSIS:

COMMENTS:

RECOMMEND	CONSIDER	PASS
	X	

HEADER

Underneath the company logo, the first section of any report focuses on the meta data regarding the submission. Title, author, genre of the script, etc. Here's a selection of other info that's often included:

Title:	Location:
Author:	Circa:
Format: Feature/TV Pilot/Podcast/Short	Budget: Low/Med/High
Page Count:	Coverage Date:
Genre:	Reader:

You may also have SUB TO: and SUB BY: in the header, which is used to indicate which company the script has been submitted to and by whom.

LOGLINE

You will usually be required to include a logline, which is one or two short sentences that sum up the entire movie. Even if you're provided with the writer's own logline, you'll need to construct your own, based on the material you read.

SYNOPSIS

Depending on the length of report you're writing, you may need to include a synopsis. This can run anything from one paragraph to 1-2 full pages long and should retell the A-story beat-by-beat, or act-by act.

COMMENTS

This is where the reader provides analysis, looking at the key elements that make up a script. Again, depending on the length of report and who it's for, i.e. the writer or a development company, comments can be as brief or as in-depth as you like when detailing what works, what doesn't, and why.

A lot of coverage companies will ask you to write comments under specific headings, such as premise, character, dialogue, etc. This can be helpful, but it can also be rather constricting too. More experienced writers often find it hard to 'pick the right box' to write their comment in, as they understand that all of the elements are interconnected. The pacing could be slowed by too much dialogue, for example, or the lack of big stakes for a character results in a weak structure, etc.

It's easier (and quicker) to write coverage without the restriction of having to write comments under individual categories, allowing notes to flow more easily, but understandably, this may not be an option for everyone. Judging which comments to place where will come with experience.

RATING

You'll also need to mark the script (and/or the writer) as a PASS, CONSIDER, or RECOMMEND. It may take you some time as a reader to figure out what constitutes a great script compared to a good script, but it's extremely rare for screenplays to be recommended, so be wary of checking that box too often.

GRADE/SCORE

Not every script coverage uses a rating grid, which should be considered as more of a visual aid for the writer to indicate which areas are already competent and which need more attention than a set-in-stone assessment. This could be in checkbox form, as below, or you may be asked to rate each element on a scale of 1 to 10, 1 to 100, or out of 5 stars, etc.

	EXCELLENT	GOOD	FAIR	POOR
PREMISE		X		
STORY			X	
CHARACTERS			X	
STRUCTURE				X
DIALOGUE		X		
MARKETABILITY			X	
WRITER			X	

The wording on this can vary. There may be "NEEDS ATTENTION" instead of "POOR", or "COMPETENT" instead of "GOOD", for example.

CHARACTER BREAKDOWNS

You won't generally be tasked with filling out a short blurb about each of the characters from a script, but this could be required for agency or management company coverage. A blurb can range from anything from a short description that matches the one given in the screenplay to a more detailed summary that includes character arcs or potential casting choices.

There are more examples of what a coverage reports should look like here:
https://www.scriptreaderscheatsheet.com/readerresources
but it's not something to get too hung up about. A writer is going to be much more interested in what you've got to say about their screenplay than the presentation of the coverage report.

LOGLINE

In most cases, you'll be required to write a logline for the script you're writing coverage on. This isn't always easy, especially when there are pivotal elements missing from the story, but this can actually be very useful when trying to point out major flaws in the writing.

In some cases, you may have access to the logline that the writer wrote themselves. This is a great way to gauge a writer's level of ability even before you read the script, as a poorly crafted logline can also be a handy indicator of what key elements are going to be missing from the script. Reading the writer's logline can also be of benefit when assessing how long the script takes to deliver the "promise of the premise". If the protagonist (aka the MC) hasn't encountered the central conflict mentioned in the logline by the end of Act I, then you'll know to include notes regarding this.

It's not your job to make the premise more appealing by crafting a logline that helps to sell the project or to embellish it into what you *think* the writer was going for yet didn't quite make it, but it is your job to use the logline to show the writer which main points are coming across from their script, and which ones aren't.

So, how do you write a logline quickly?

Try one of these formulas, using only the information delivered in the screenplay. There's room to mix and match elements here, so figure out which best accurately summarizes the plot.

1. Protagonist + Goal + Problem
2. Protagonist + Problem + Stakes
3. Protagonist + Goal + Stakes
4. Setup + Protagonist + Goal + Problem
5. Protagonist + Character Flaw + Goal

Protagonist: Don't include the MC's (main character) name here unless the script is a biopic. Write a summary of who the main story is about, such as 'a loyal toy cowboy', 'a Scottish heroin addict', 'an off-duty cop', or 'four teenage boys on the cusp of adulthood'.

Goal: This is what the MC is trying to achieve rather than what's getting in the way of them achieving it. 'desperately trying to get home', 'must overcome a past trauma', 'has to help a friendly alien return to their home planet', or 'survive a plane crash on a freezing mountaintop'.

Problem: Although there may be several different problems occurring as the story unfolds, concentrate on the initial conflict that arises from the inciting incident which propels the MC on their journey, such as 'a man-eating shark terrorizing the community', 'can't tell a lie for 24 hours', 'is unknowingly stuck in a reality TV show', or 'have unwittingly let a dangerous alien on-board their spacecraft'.

Stakes: This explains what's at risk should the primary goal fail. If the writer has weak stakes in their plot, this is a good place to highlight that. Stakes can be both physical and emotional, such as 'stopping a murderer whose next target is the MC's own family', 'risks losing the respect of his young son', or 'being stranded on a desert island forever'.

Setup: Sometimes a logline will need some context to help it make sense, such as 'in a post-apocalyptic future', 'while conducting research at a remote Antarctica outpost', or 'after an android is sent from the future'. If the story is set in a unique place and it adds to the conflict, it may be worth including it in the logline too.

Character Flaw: This can be especially helpful when writing a logline for a drama, where the antagonistic force might be more of a personal struggle for the MC to overcome, but is also a great element to add regardless, such as 'an insomniac office worker', 'a mentally unstable taxi driver', or 'a womanizing out-of-work actor'. Adding a character flaw, weakness, or limitation can help heighten a logline, such as 'a local sheriff with a fear of the sea (who must save his community from a killer shark)' or 'a wheelchair-bound woman (who must find a way to scale back down Everest after the rest of her climbing crew are killed)'.

As you can see, there are lots of ways to write a logline, but primarily focus on who the story is about, what they're trying to achieve, why it's important that they succeed, and what's standing in their way.

SYNOPSIS

A synopsis, or brief summary of the plot, may or may not be required in your report, but it is a useful way to show writers which story beats are clear, and which aren't. Depending on how much space you have to fill, a synopsis can be anything from one short paragraph to 1-2 full pages. Breaking a synopsis into smaller, manageable paragraphs to indicate acts or sequences will make it easier for both you and the writer to see where the major story beats are. Focus primarily on the MC's journey by outlining the goal, activity, and problems that occur within each act.

You need to represent the script as it's written, meaning that there's no room to add your own embellishments, presumptions, or impressions. Try to emulate the tone that came across in the script here, too. You should be trying to show the script in its best light regardless of the quality of the writing, so stick to focusing on the main plotline and ignore any subplots concerning minor characters unless they become key points in the main story. Also include selected quotations from the script if you need to highlight a strong beat, line of dialogue, or emotional moment.

PREMISE

The premise (or concept) is essentially what the main story is about. It's the core concept from which the logline can be derived, and it's the most important element when assessing whether or not a script will sell. Ultimately, a badly written script that's based on a great idea is going to be much more valuable than a well-crafted screenplay that's boring.

Always start with praise, so don't delve straight into which areas are weakest and need attention. Highlight what worked and why. If the writer is new, there's every chance the script will be terrible, but always place the focus on its potential and what the script *could* be if it was developed further. Who might it appeal to and why? What strong themes does it contain? Is it relevant? Is there a gap in the market it could exploit? If possible, draw comparisons to similar movies or material, highlighting why they were (or weren't) successful and how they relate to the script you're reading.

Try not to waste too much time regurgitating the plot back to the writer in this section, even if you haven't included a synopsis in the report. That's sloppy coverage. The writer hasn't paid you to tell them what they already know they've written.

When assessing a TV pilot or web-series pilot, a reader usually isn't privy to any supporting material, such as a series outline, treatment, or pitch, and they'll have to assess the potential of the series from the pilot script alone. While this can make the job slightly harder, often, if a pilot script contains too many unanswered questions, there's the risk that potential viewers won't bother waiting for the next episode to find the answers, which should be highlighted to the writer. There's a fine line between mystery and reveal that you need to assess in cases like this.

> **CHEATS**
>
> There's a compelling, heavily thematic story here with instantly likable characters being thrust into a gripping conflict, all of which helps to create a standout script.
>
> This piece has plenty of appeal, almost having a "why hasn't this been done before?" feel to it.

> **CHEATS CONT.**
>
> This script ticks all the right boxes when it comes to crafting a marketable, relevant, and relatable modern (genre) piece.
>
> This low-budget piece may have a minimal cast, but it has maximum conflict and will be very appealing to producers.
>
> Reminiscent of (similar already produced material), this script could do well to (fill the gap in the market/ride on the success of/feed an eager fanbase, etc.)

TITLE

A reader will generally never need to write any comments about the title of a screenplay, as it's probably considered the least important element of a script. Any recommendations to change one should instead come from the marketing or sales department (if the script sells, that is!), but there are a couple of instances where you may need to give a writer the heads up if something really isn't working.

Consider making a comment if;

THE TITLE IS MISLEADING

Producers could easily have been forgiven for thinking that *Pineapple Express* (2008) was a colorful cartoon for kids or that *Trainspotting* (1996) was anything other than a black comedy about heroin addiction, so if the title doesn't fit the genre or isn't suggestive of the premise, there's the small chance it could be dismissed before it's even read. It's unlikely, but why risk it, right?

If the title doesn't immediately evoke the premise or genre of the piece, not only is there the possibility that producers could overlook it, there's an even greater chance that potential audiences might disregard it too. Viewers scrolling through dozens of movie titles might ignore a misleading title, making it more difficult to market a script towards its intended target audience. Point out the risks if you think that a title is giving off completely the wrong vibe.

CHEATS

A much more effective title that evokes the genre and plot would help to increase the marketability of the piece.
At present, there's the risk that genre fans may overlook this movie/TV series as the title's not quite suggestive enough of (the intended genre).
Be aware that the current title is more evocative of (suggested genre) than (actual genre), which has the potential to mislead.
It's possibly worth revising the title of the piece, as there's the risk that it may mislead both potential audiences and prospective producers. Try to evoke the genre or premise more if possible.

THE TITLE COULD CAUSE OFFENCE

As far as first impressions go, a title that is insulting to the reader, to a specific group of people, or is widely regarded as offensive, probably isn't the best way to sell a spec script. Having shock value can certainly work well to grab people's attention, so there may be method in the madness, but it also makes a movie harder to market, so advise the writer of this if you see any potentially derogatory or unnecessarily provocative wording in the title.

CHEATS

While the title is certainly eye-catching, there is a slight chance that it could have a detrimental effect when pitching this project.
Be careful not to make pitching this project unnecessarily difficult by having a potentially offensive title.
It could be worth using a temporary alternative title while pitching in order to ensure that the present title doesn't stop anyone from turning away the script before reading it.

GENRE

Strong genre pieces sell well, as do well-written hybrids, but the boundaries continue to soften and the number of sub-genres is growing, so it's not uncommon to see a successful movie be listed as several different genres at the same time. A writer needs to understand who their audience is, what expectations that audience has when watching, and how to deliver something fresh and exciting. Adhering to genre conventions can both help and hinder a writer, so you must be able to recognize what works and what doesn't.

Consider making a comment if;

GENRE IS UNCLEAR

A writer not generating the right tone, missing essential tropes, using too many elements from too many genres, or the genre elements being too weak or infrequent are all factors that might make it difficult to determine exactly what genre a script is categorized as. If it's hard to see which genre the writer is going for, it's also possible that they're trying to make their story fit into the wrong genre, in which case, you need to advise that the writer considers which genre(s) would best suit their story.

It's perfectly fine for a script to be more than one genre. Mixing genres can be an effective way to create something fresh, memorable, and add life to old ideas, but if the genre of a script is unclear, it makes it hard for a studio to market it, meaning they might not want to take a risk on a screenplay that doesn't have a clearly defined audience. Point out that adhering to one or two clear genres will help make the script easier to sell. If the script combines two genres that slightly clash or don't mesh together well and there's the potential for it to move more in one direction than the other, push the writer into making a final decision on which genre to commit to by highlighting which is the stronger genre to use, which is more marketable, or which is going to create a more exciting and rewarding story for the audience.

It's important that the genre, or sub-genre, is established clearly during the first act of the script (as well as being maintained throughout too, of course) as this helps viewers understand what to expect. If no crime has been committed during the first act of a crime mystery, for example, then the writer probably needs advice on speeding up the pace or rearranging the structure. If the scene description is bland or matter-of-factly in a children's action adventure script, then advise the writer to use tone to help establish the genre more strongly. Or if a script is cluttered with too many genres mashed together, it could be that the writer is trying to make their movie accessible to as wide an audience as possible, but in trying to please everyone, they risk satisfying no one.

> **CHEATS**
>
> At present, it's hard to gauge what genre this script is, especially from the first (few pages/first act), where it's essential to give the reader some idea of what type of story they're reading.
>
> At this stage, it's not clear which genre this script fits into, making it essential that the writer figures out who the intended audience is, what they'll want and what they won't want, in order to ensure that they provide a rewarding experience.
>
> Think carefully about who the target audience is here. Is the writing doing enough to fulfill their expectations or could the lack of commitment to any one genre risk leaving them feeling unsatisfied?

IT DOESN'T ADD ANYTHING NEW TO THE GENRE

Genre conventions are essentially various archetypes, plots, actions, or expectations that have developed over time and they're integral to specific genres. Conventions (and tropes) are a great tool to help deliver information faster, but over time, certain conventions have been used so often, they could now be regarded as being cliché. The first time someone wrote the 'monster' being dealt a mortal blow that they couldn't possibly survive only to resurface for the climactic showdown mere moments later did a fantastic job of creating a new and unexpected twist to the slasher genre, but that trope has now been used so many times, it's almost expected, meaning that it's also fairly predictable, and predictable means boring.

If you're reading a script where it's easy to see where the plot is heading, the characters take every expected action, have foreseeable reactions, and the ending was predictable from the beginning, you could suggest that the writer tries to experiment more with breaking genre conventions, delivering something unexpected, using more unfamiliar tropes, or creating something that has the potential to become a new convention altogether.

> **CHEATS**
>
> The piece contains plenty of genre conventions, but there's also scope to experiment more with audience expectations to provide the unexpected, to keep the viewers guessing, and to minimize the predictability.
>
> Now would be a good time to question what this script is giving audiences that they haven't already seen before. If that's a hard question to answer, get creative and look for moments in the script where something unexpected could occur or for ways to move the story off in surprising new directions.
>
> This is a great homage to the (genre type) movies that have gone before, but try to avoid predictable cliches by giving the piece its own unique spin, to surprise the audience, and to bring something new to the genre.
>
> Although (positive comment), is this script really giving us something viewers haven't ever seen before or could it be relying too much on established genre expectations and conventions?
>
> We've all seen the (worn out trope), the (cliche), and the (overused genre convention), so figure out a way to put a new spin on these elements to help make them feel fresh, new, and exciting.

THERE AREN'T ENOUGH GENRE CONVENTIONS

It's quite simple, a horror has to horrify its viewers, a drama needs to have lots of emotional conflict, action movies need to contain several high-octane and inventive action sequences, comedies need to be consistently funny, and thrillers need to keep the audience on their toes, but all too often, you'll read a script that claims to be a certain genre yet doesn't quite deliver on the fundamentals. Most commonly, a drama script doesn't contain enough drama, there's no suspense, twists or red-herrings in a supposed thriller, there's a distinct lack of laughs in a script marked as a comedy, and having only one cowboy in a script doesn't mean that it's a western, etc.

If a script doesn't contain enough genre conventions, it won't satisfy the audience. Highlight what's perhaps missing from the writer's script at the same time as pointing out the few instances where they did manage to hit the nail on the head in order to give encouragement. What conventions did they use that they can build further upon? It's possible that the writer doesn't understand what genre they're trying to write in, that they only have some interesting scenes loosely linked together, or that the story just isn't engaging enough. In each case, advise that they commit to one (or two) clear genres to help make the script more marketable, to knit the story tighter together, which in turn, will help the writer find audience-pleasing moments that make their story more compelling.

CHEATS

This is essentially a (genre) with no (genre conventions), which could make it difficult to market this script, which in turn makes it harder to sell.

When (genre) fans go to see a (genre) movie, they expect (genre conventions). At present, there aren't enough occurring in this script, which risks leaving viewers unsatisfied.

Could adding in some well-known tropes and genre conventions help enhance the script by fulfilling more audience expectations and increase its marketability too?

It's worth doing a little more research on how to adhere to genre here. Strong genre pieces sell well and understanding what the target audience is expecting will not only help deliver a more satisfying experience; it'll also create room to play with those expectations too.

THEME

While the premise is what the story is about, theme is what the story is *really* about. It's the purpose of the story; the feelings and emotions a writer is trying to evoke and the universal statement about the human condition that they're trying to make. Trying to decipher what the overarching theme or message is behind a story is can be difficult, especially if the writer isn't sure themselves, but as it's something that should be present in almost every scene of a screenplay, when it isn't, it might be detrimental to the overall story.

Consider making a comment if;

THE OVERALL THEME OR MESSAGE IS UNCLEAR

You'll often be able to tell when a script contains strong themes, but when there's no definitive core motif or message behind the story, you may be left with a "what was the point of that?" feeling, and if you, the reader, feels this way, there's a big chance that the audience will feel the same way too.

Ideally, there should be an action, line of dialogue, or question being asked during the first act that establishes the central theme, so this is your starting point when looking for one, but theme can be a difficult area for writers to get to grips with, and not every writer will know what the theme of their story is. It's often something that they come to discover during or after writing the script, but if you feel the story lacks any purpose, ask the writer to consider why they wanted to tell this particular story in the first place, what is it about the story that makes it an important one to tell, what do they want the audience to take away after watching it, and what fundamental question is their story asking? Only once the writer has figured out their theme can they make sure it's incorporated into every scene in their screenplay.

CHEATS

While there's (positive comment), at this stage, with no strong character arc occurring for (the MC), it's a little difficult to figure out what the overall message of the story is.

Consider stating the theme verbally during the first act (often by a secondary character) to ensure that the reader can effectively pinpoint thematically charged moments in the script, as at present, it's not entirely clear what the central theme is here.

At this stage, the theme isn't quite coming through strongly enough. Don't worry, it's not uncommon for writers to have discovered what the theme is until well into the rewriting process. Look at the lessons that (the MC) learns during their journey and figure out what big question they've answered by the end in order to find it.

THERE ARE TOO MANY THEMES

Occasionally, you'll read a script that contains lots of big themes. These are often big blockbusters, epics, TV series, or sci-fi movies, where there's an ensemble cast, lots of subplots/story threads, or multiple narratives. It's more common for feature scripts to have just one big central theme with some smaller sub-themes that look at subtle variations, but sometimes writers don't quite get the balance right when trying to tackle too many big issues.

If there are too many themes being explored, you'll need to assess whether some are taking precious screen time away from others, which themes are going to be less entertaining, therefore making them potential cuts, or whether some themes could be knitted together more tightly if they clash. If the plot feels muddled thanks to too many themes, ask the writer to figure out which theme they believe is the strongest and advise that they either focus on that one single theme, or that they make sure that the other sub-themes are at least strongly connected in some manner to the central theme as well.

CHEATS

Thematically, there's a lot going on, and while that can often enhance a story, some of the themes in this script are clashing with others, pulling the audience's focus in too many different directions.

With several themes running throughout this script, try to figure out which one is going to resonate most with the audience, which is the most interesting, or which explores the theme in the most unique manner. Consider placing all of the focus on the strongest theme instead of spreading multiple themes too thinly.

Consider dialling things back and focusing solely on one powerful theme rather than trying to cram too many smaller ones into the script. This will de-clutter the story and allow more time for character development.

Thematically, (first theme) is the most interesting, but there's the sense that (second theme) and/or (third theme) are taking precious screen time away from that theme being fully explored.

THEME ISN'T REFLECTED IN THE SUBPLOTS

A plot that has several themes can make a script read more like a series of disjointed smaller stories that aren't particularly well connected, as opposed to a well-crafted central story with multiple threads that all tie neatly together. There are various types of subplots a writer can use, but they all work best when they're connected to the main story via theme. Subplots can be used to look at theme from another perspective, through minor characters, or by adding another layer of conflict, but when this isn't happening, subplots can begin to feel like unnecessary distractions from the main plot or worse, as space-filler content on the page.

Encourage the writer to re-examine any subplot that isn't particularly adding anything to the main plot and ask them to look for ways to better connect it by either adding setups that are later paid off in the main plot (or vice versa), having the conflict within the subplot be a variation of the central theme, or using it to explore the theme via a personal struggle for whichever minor characters are present in that thread.

CHEATS
There's scope to tighten the script further by thematically connecting (secondary character's) side quest to (the MC's) primary goal.
At present, (secondary character's) plot thread feels too separate from the main plot and that makes it a potential cut. To ensure this subplot stays in the script, consider knitting both together using the central theme to bind them.
Consider using the subplots to further explore the central theme, which will add depth and make the story feel more layered. What opposing argument could also be present in a subplot? How does (secondary character) deal with a similar emotional problem to (the MC)? Are any minor characters facing similar conflicts, etc.?

THE THEME DOESN'T GET RESOLVED

If the main theme is asking a question, such as 'can a man and a woman really just be friends?' as used in *When Harry Met Sally* (1989), but that question doesn't get answered by the end of the movie, then there's going to be plenty of unsatisfied viewers. Open-ended stories carry the same risk, but sometimes there are themes that are just too big and complex to have a simple answer that will please, so take that into consideration when commenting. If the theme is more of a statement than a question, such as 'sacrifice', but the protagonist doesn't redeem themselves by putting it all on the line by the end of the script, or if the theme is 'survival', but everyone dies at the end, then there's going to be mixed reactions by viewers expecting a more rewarding outcome.

Get the writer to focus on what overall feeling they want the audience to leave with after watching their movie. If they want to create a shocking, unexpected ending, that's fine, as long as they're aware of the potential risks in doing so, but if they've started their story by asking a central question or statement and they don't answer or conclude it, then it begs the question, why ask it in the first place?

CHEATS

If this is a story about (possible theme), then that needs to be resolved by the end of the story in order to ensure a rewarding experience for the audience.

Consider what question the story is posing or what opinion about life is being explored and whether the ending provides an adequate conclusion. If it's unclear what central question is being asked here, more attention should be given to what the overall theme is. Knowing this will help determine whether the ending is going to be fulfilling enough for the audience.

The thematic question that was posed at the beginning seems to get forgotten about by the end. Keeping the emotional response that's trying to be generated in the audience during the third act in mind, consider resolving the theme in some manner to help provide an adequate conclusion.

TONE

Tone is the atmosphere, the feeling, or the mood that the piece gives off and it's a great tool to help convey genre too. It's how a writer elicits emotion in the audience, and as a writer can use just about every element of a screenplay to help control tone, such as dialogue, scene description, imagery, and action, it's a powerful instrument to wield. Although the tone can change throughout a script, a writer needs to establish the initial tone or mood during the first act, ideally within the first few pages.

Consider making a comment if;

THE TONE ISN'T IMMEDIATELY CLEAR

Setting the tone is important. It tells the audience what type of story to expect and that helps to cut down on the amount of setup needed. If there's nothing funny, light-hearted, or amusing happening in the early scenes of a comedy, if there's no anticipation, tension, or suspense being created in the opening of a thriller, or there's no sense of foreboding, anxiety, or dread arising at the beginning of a horror (of course, this could be the writer using misdirection or setting up a surprise twist, in which case it's fine) then it's likely that the writer is having issues conveying tone.

There are a few different places that a writer can use to better establish tone at the beginning of their script; but primarily ask them to focus on visual elements, such as the opening image, the setting, and the way they introduce the MC to the viewers. What first visual could they use that would help evoke the mood? Is there a different location that would better suggest the atmosphere? And what action could the MC be taking, or is involved in, that would leave the audience in no doubt as to what genre they're watching, etc.? Once they're able to establish tone using visual imagery, then encourage them to use word choice and selective sentence structure to evoke tone in their writing too.

> ### CHEATS
>
> Do more to set the tone during those all-important first few pages. Just as action and dialogue can be used to set the tone, scene description should also be used to evoke atmosphere and mood too.
>
> It's not until (specific action) happens that it becomes clear that this is a (genre) script, and leaving it this late risks lulling the reader/audience into a false sense of security. While that can be very effective when attempting to shock/surprise, there's also the chance that viewers tune out beforehand, or worse, feel cheated.

> **CHEATS CONT.**
>
> Try to establish the tone and mood of the piece via action, dialogue, and evocative scene description as early as on page one. This helps generate audience expectations and can help cut back on the need for excessive setup, too.

TONE ISN'T STRONG ENOUGH

There's a difference between a writer's voice and a writer's tone, so be careful not to confuse the two. Tone isn't what a writer is saying, it's how they say it, and if there's a lack of tone in someone's writing, then there's every chance that it's bland, uninspiring, or emotionless, all of which significantly lessen a reader's ability to connect with it, which is exactly what a spec script needs to be doing.

Music plays a big part in creating tone while we're watching a movie or TV show, but obviously, a writer can't rely on this device in their script. Encourage writers to use selective word choice, setting, vivid imagery, the order they reveal information, and character to help evoke tone. Get the writer to shift their focus from just telling us what's happening on screen to how they want the reader to react to it. Reading other screenplays, as well as novels, is a big recommendation here if tone is a particular weakness for the writer, as delivering tone is all about knowing how to engage with the reader and that's best learned via the first-hand experience of reading.

> **CHEATS**
>
> Consider enriching the writing even further by reflecting the tone using every element available on the page. Tone isn't just created by action and dialogue; scene description and headings can also evoke atmosphere and mood if desired too.
>
> Don't forget, a script needs to be just as engaging to read as it will be to watch, so consider using the scene description to reflect both the tone and genre here, too.
>
> What's not coming through as strongly as it could be is the tone. Try to use evocative wording throughout the script to help conjure up the desired emotions in the audience.

TONE IS INCONSISTENT

We're not talking about small tonal shifts throughout a story here, such as some comic relief or a quiet moment that's used to let you catch your breath in between a high-octane action sequence. These 'breaks' in the overall tone can work extremely well to enhance the pace and satisfaction of a story, but if the tone changes too frequently or too drastically, it can cause confusion for the audience and it can also lessen the believability of a story too.

If a script begins off as a slapstick comedy but then transitions into a serious thriller, not only is it going to be hard to market it towards the right audience, it'll also make it harder to sell the script. The writer also risks ruining any audience expectations they've built up, meaning that they'll need to spend more time than necessary on their setup in order to make sure that the change in tone doesn't make the viewers lose interest or make the story difficult to believe.

Indicate to the writer that when they're first establishing the tone, they're telling the audience what type of story to expect, and if they don't deliver on that promise, they risk leaving the audience feeling somewhat cheated. An inconsistent tone also risks a writer coming across as not knowing what type of story they're trying to tell, or that they're trying to please too wide an audience, so it's certainly something to avoid. Advise they do a tone pass, concentrating on keeping the tone as consistent throughout as possible.

CHEATS

It's not unusual for the tone to shift throughout a story as a writer tries to manipulate the audience's reaction, but at certain points during this read, the tonal shift might be considered too jarring and this risks hampering the dramatic momentum that's being built and it lessens the (emotion) trying to be evoked in the viewers.

The shift from (first tone) to (second tone) during (specific sequence) has a jarring effect that could prevent the audience from becoming engrossed in the action, so it's worth considering exactly what emotions are trying to be roused in the viewers at that point and whether the tone needs to be adjusted in order to achieve that.

> **CHEATS CONT.**
>
> There's a bizarre mix of tones throughout the script. Sometimes it's (slapstick/informal/optimistic, etc.) and at others, it's (threatening/serious/pessimistic, etc.), which makes it hard to gauge which target audience is trying to be pleased here. There's scope to take the script in both directions here, so figure out who the primary audience is and which tone best suits their needs.

ORIGINALITY

We've all heard the 'give us the same, but different' quote when talking about what studios and execs are looking for in a spec script, but with so much having previously gone before, it's no small task for a writer to produce something that's both familiar and new. No one likes to be told that their screenplay isn't original, but sometimes even though the writing itself may be good, if the story is nothing but a blatant re-hash of past concepts, it's ultimately going to make the script harder to sell. Here, it's important to get writers to come to the realization themselves by posing some pivotal questions that get them thinking.

Consider making a comment if;

IT'S TOO SIMILAR TO ALREADY PRODUCED MATERIAL

Point out that it's clear that the story was heavily influenced by other work(s), but there's a thin line between writing an homage and simply copying previously released movies. Regardless of whether the writing is enjoyable with an MC we want to root for, the script may be guilty of using too many clichés that make the plot fairly predictable. In cases like this, it's hard to see what the script is giving us that we haven't seen countless times before. While not impossible to sell, it's unlikely to satisfy viewers or genre fans.

It's not your job to tell writers how to be more creative, but you can point them in the right direction. There are many ways to inject a little originality into a plot, from swapping the genders and ages of the characters, setting a familiar story in a unique location, to playing with audience expectations and inserting more unexpected twists and turns into the plotline.

> **CHEATS**
>
> Although there's a good attempt to explore different aspects of a strong universal theme here, are there enough original elements, and will this movie stand out amongst others already in the same genre?
>
> At present, the piece is possibly just too similar to what's currently already out there, making this a difficult script to sell. Consider putting a more unique stamp on the characters, events, and scenarios. Could mixing up genders, adding diversity, changing the time period or setting help put a new spin on an old idea?
>
> The problem with trends is that once something's been shown on screen, that trend has already passed. It's not a bad thing to jump on the bandwagon, but a writer needs to be extremely fast. Smaller independent studios may very well be looking for material they believe will have a guaranteed audience, but consider which is going to be more impressive and helpful in terms of advancing a writers career, an original concept, or a re-hash of already made material?
>
> At this stage, there are just too many copyrighted elements being used in the script. Do more to make those elements less identifiable, more unique, and turn them into unique creations in order to avoid any potential legal action being taken.

IT'S SO UNCONVENTIONAL, IT'S CONFUSING

Sometimes you'll encounter a writer that's attempted to break just about every rule in the book, which results in a script that's just so off-the-wall that it's confusing, hard to digest, and ultimately, unenjoyable to read. What can initially come across as trying to be original is really just poor execution of screenwriting fundamentals, and what the writer has in imagination is unfortunately lacking in craft, as it's primarily newbie writers you'll see doing this.

There's nothing wrong with breaking the rules, as long as it works to enhance the story, but realistically, studios and execs aren't going to take a big financial risk by backing a new writer with no previous credits, writing experience, or one who probably needs to learn to walk before they can run. Symptoms of this are a writer not really adhering to genre conventions, having unbelievable characters, having no clear plot, or hard to follow dialogue, so encourage the writer to reel it back in and to concentrate more on whichever basics need the most work in order to add more of the 'familiar' to their unique story.

> **CHEATS**
>
> There's a lot going on in this script, which is a testament to the writers' creative ability, but at present, it can be very difficult to keep up with the story, and if a script is confusing to read, it's going to be extremely hard to sell.
>
> With so many (plot threads/characters/themes/world-building elements, etc.) it can be extremely difficult to keep track of what's going on. Pulling things back, focusing on one central (theme/thread/character, etc.), and keeping it simple would help to make the story much more digestible, making the script much more enjoyable to read too.
>
> The story feels as though it's very much still in the writer's head than down on the page, with (time jumps/missing details/inconsistent character names/unbelievable actions, etc.) that creates too much confusion. It's important to make everything as clear as possible in order to enhance the read rather than complicate it, so consider going back to the beat sheet to plot (the MC's) journey linearly, keeping the focus on believability and the emotions trying to be evoked in the audience along the way.

THE STORY IS BASED ON THE WRITERS BORING LIFE

There's absolutely nothing wrong with someone 'writing what they know' and taking inspiration from their own life when telling a story, but unfortunately, not everyone has a cinema-worthy life story to tell. This doesn't mean that stories like this can't find a market elsewhere, as intimate, emotional, personal experience stories often work well on the smaller screen or as short films, so understanding which audience would suit the material will help here, but ultimately just because a personal story is important to the writer, doesn't necessarily mean that it's going to be interesting to anyone else.

A big giveaway is if the protagonist shares the same name as the writer, or there's a "based on real events" quote written on the title page, and there's often going to be a distinct lack of conflict, drama, or strong story beats in the script too. Focus on how to help the writer make their script more marketable. What small moments could they turn into bigger cinematic ones? Does the writer need to distance themselves a little more from the MC in order to make them more likeable, relatable, empathic, etc., or does the core idea need something extra to help it become high concept?

CHEATS

Not everyone's personal story is cinematic enough for the big screen, but that doesn't mean it's not a story worth telling. At present, this low-concept idea could find more success as a (short film/TV series/fiction podcast, etc.) than as a feature film, so it's certainly worth considering adapting the piece into a different medium.

Just because something happened in real life doesn't automatically make it interesting to watch, so paying close attention to the dramatic momentum that's happening throughout the story is essential here.

Every scene needs to include stakes or conflict. If they don't, they're potential cuts, regardless of whether they happened in real life or not. Make sure that every scene is serving a purpose, is entertaining, and is moving the plot forward, otherwise, they're potential cuts.

A writer has an artistic license to bend the truth, add conflicts where there were none, and heighten the emotion in order to create an engaging story that keeps the audience wanting more. Don't feel that it's necessary to stay true to real life at all times, especially during scenes that aren't moving the story forward in any manner.

THE STORY IS A BORING FACT-BASED ADAPTATION

Biopics, along with adaptations, have for a long time been prominent Oscar winners, making them a popular genre for writers to attempt, but often a writer can struggle to understand what information to include and what to omit when adapting a novel or real-life story for the screen.

When looking at biopics, a writer needs to remember that just because something happened in real life, doesn't mean it'll make an entertaining story to watch. There still needs to be conflict, engaging characters, a compelling hook etc., and it can become easy for a writer to want to include absolutely everything, from a character's birth right up to their death, but often, the only story-worthy content occurs during a small period during someone's life.

If a writer has started their story too early, encourage them to learn how to filter out which parts of someone's life story are essential to the script, which are hindering the pace, which don't reveal anything new or interesting, and which aren't strongly connected to the central theme.

Not only do writer's need to figure out the best place to start and end their story, they should also be encouraged to use their artistic license whenever they need to turn a boring, but necessary, exposition scene into something more entertaining, dramatic, visual, or emotional. Writers are allowed to bend the truth, but the important factor is that it helps add to the story in some manner.

When dealing with adaptations, the writer again may feel as though they have to include everything that happened in the book and they end up with a script that over runs in length, has too many subplots, too many characters, or over-relies on narration or voice over to tell the story. Not every book can or should be adapted for the screen.

CHEATS

It can be extremely difficult when deciding what to keep and what to cut when adapting material, so keeping the dramatic momentum in mind is pivotal. Make sure that every scene contains stakes or conflict to ensure that it's serving a purpose.

Be careful not to clutter the page with unnecessary details that hinder both the pace of the story and the read. Only tell us pivotal info that's helping to move the plot forward. If it's not essential that we know (list specific examples here), then it shouldn't be taking up space in the script.

At times, the pacing suffers due to too many filler scenes where (information is being repeated/the plot isn't moving forward/nothing new is being delivered, etc.) and while the writer may be trying to stay true to the original material here, these types of scenes don't translate to the screen very well.

> **CHEATS CONT.**
>
> Keep the viewers who aren't already familiar with the subject matter in mind while writing too. Is there enough continual drama, conflict, and high stakes to keep them engaged, or is too much being thrown at them here? There's a limited time in a screenplay to tell the story, so know when to use the gripping moments over the factually correct yet uninteresting ones.

MEDIUM

Scripts come in all shapes and sizes, but unfortunately, if the peg doesn't fit the hole the writer is trying to force it into, they could have a tough time selling it. You'll need to assess whether a script might lean more towards a certain genre, whether the concept has legs, and where best to find its intended target audience.

Make sure you know what's happening in current markets. Half-hour dramas or thrillers never used to be a thing, but with the increase of streaming services and the appetite for binge-watching, there's now a market for shorter formats, meaning that scripts that were previously no-no's, are now selling. There's also a blur in what it now means to be a sitcom, with stories no longer being confined to a multi-camera studio setup, there's a lot more freedom, but remember that certain genres still have expectations, rules, and restrictions.

Consider making a comment if;

IT DOESN'T FIT THE CHOSEN FORMAT

It's easier to spot this in scripts that have an awkward page count. Take a 43-page TV script, for example. It would be hard to find a slot in a broadcast schedule for something of this length, making it a hard sell. You need to decide if the concept has potential to be developed into a half-hour show or a one-hour drama. A lot depends on whether there's room to add in more plot, if there's lots of fluff that can easily be cut out, or whether the story is solid enough, in which case the writer should start targeting online content creators.

It can be difficult for a reader to interpret the intention of a script, especially with no further information about the project other than the screenplay itself. A script for a short film might read more like a proof of concept for a longer piece, a feature script could work better divided up into shorter stream-able episodes, or a one-hour television drama may be high concept enough that it would have a better chance of selling if it was fleshed out into a movie, etc.

A standalone short film that finds itself a little on the longer side might be better marketed as a series if the concept has enough legs to carry it. A feature length script that has a large cast, contains lots of story threads, and themes, may also work better if it was developed into a television series, so that enough time could be devoted to exploring the characters and world.

Sometimes it's difficult to assess whether a screenplay has been written to be filmed as an animation or as a live-action piece, especially with family-friendly fantasy stories, so it might be useful to highlight to the writer that firstly, they have a piece that's potentially attractive to two different types of producers, and secondly, mention whether the script might lean more towards one than the other and why. Changing the format is ultimately a decision for the writer to make, so there's no need to force the point, but suggesting other avenues that may suit the project better will at least allow the writer to consider other options.

CHEATS

With the script coming (under/over) the desired page count, is (the current format) the best medium for this story?

Consider whether adapting the (current format) into (alternative format) might increase the script's chances of getting produced. (detail the advantages that changing the format might bring).

This is an impressive and ambitious piece, which works well as a sample that has potential when entering contests, but producers and execs are less likely to take a big financial risk on a relatively new writer. Adapting this script into a (shorter or serialized format) could help minimize that risk and increase the chances of getting this script made.

THE CONCEPT DOESN'T HAVE LEGS

This applies more to web and television series than it does to feature scripts unless the writer is hoping to develop a franchise, but when pitching to a producer or exec, the more seasons they think they can stretch a concept into, the more chance there is of selling it. It can be difficult to assess this from one script alone as any information regarding the content of future episodes or the series arc is something that would be included in the series pitch or bible rather than the actual screenplay, but if the pilot episode wraps everything up too tightly, doesn't plant any setups to be paid off in later episodes, doesn't have characters you'd want to tune in to watch again, uses up all the expected jokes and tropes in the one episode, or has a poor end of episode hook, then you may need to advise the writer that their script might not have the appeal it should.

There could be any number of factors that leave a script feeling underwhelming. It could be that weak conflicts are easily resolved, there's easily solved mysteries that don't offer anymore, a will-they-won't-they relationship that concludes too quickly, so you'll need to figure out which aspects need more work to help give the sense that the concept and characters are strong enough to generate a significantly more content that will keep viewers wanting to watch.

CHEATS
The longer a series runs, the more revenue it generates, and this is why lots of producers look for concepts with legs. While not impossible, limited series do sell. Heightening or broadening the concept could make this piece more appealing, which is certainly something to consider.
Could you possibly be limiting the script's ability to get produced by making this a limited series instead of one that has the potential to run for many seasons?
At present, although there's a well-written pilot here, it's also a (contained/limited concept/restricted premise, etc.) and that could limit its appeal to (producers/studios, etc.). Would giving the premise wider audience appeal, developing the potential for more conflict, or adding more depth to the characters help give this concept enough legs to carry it for more (episodes/seasons, etc.)?

LENGTH

Page count is one of the first things that a reader looks at and it can also add to the pivotal first impression that they'll have. There's good reason why spec scripts are required to be a certain length. It shows that a writer has the discipline to condense a story into a manageable size, longer scripts need bigger budgets, and studios want movies to slot nicely into suitable running times to maximize viewership. If you're a big-name screenwriter with a body of produced work, it's fine to break these rules, but for fledgling writers trying to get a foot in the door, it's usually going to backfire.

Keeping within specific page counts also helps the reader gauge whether the writer is hitting the major story beats at roughly the right times too. If you're reading a script with an off-kilter page count, use **beatsheetcalculator.com** to figure out when each of the 15 major events that Blake Snyder established should be hitting. Snyder's beats are just one guide of many, so don't feel that a writer (or you as a reader) have to stick to them stringently here.

Consider making a comment if;

THE SCRIPT IS TOO LONG OR TOO SHORT

Certain genres, such as epics, allow for longer scripts while horror and comedies are usually on the shorter side, but the industry has the 90-120 (probably closer to 85-110 now) page rule for a reason. Anything significantly shorter probably will not be worthy of getting a cinema release and is more likely to be considered as a straight to DVD or online release instead, and anything longer risks producers and studios not wanting to risk investing in a new writer with a spec script that requires a larger budget. Length is even more important for television scripts, where shows need to fit into designated time slots and a writer needs to demonstrate that they can write to this remit.

To counter argue any writers stating that there are countless successful movies that run much longer than two-hours out there, the harsh truth is that most of those movies didn't start out as spec scripts. They were either adaptations; meaning that they already had a guaranteed audience, or were original works by well-known writer/directors with a proven body of work behind them. Studios generally won't take the risk on an unknown writer that's unable to curtail their story into the expected length.

Advise the writer that they either need to do a severe edit that cuts the story back to its bare bones, add in more content to fill out the running time, consider adapting their script to suit other formats, or dividing their script up in order to create a franchise.

CHEATS

As the script is significantly (under/over) the average page-count for a (current format), it's not meeting the required criteria. Possible solutions include (adding a new subplot/creating more character development moments/cutting unessential scenes/doing a harsh edit that minimizes the fluff, etc.).

A writer needs to prove that they can contain their story within the expected page count of whatever format they're writing in. Having a script that's massively over the 120-page maximum (or whatever the page count is for the format being used) shows a lack of discipline, but (possible solutions suggested by the reader) would help bring the page count to a more reasonable length.

The excessively (short/long) page count could suggest that the story would better suit a different format. Seriously think about whether enough content can be (added/cut) to meet the desired length.

POOR FORMATTING HAS ALTERED THE PAGE COUNT

Writers need to be made aware that for anyone who is spending every working day reading screenplays, it's immediately noticeable when the industry standard layout has been manipulated. Adjusting the margins to make a script fit into the desired page count just tells the reader that the author didn't have the ability to write efficiently and had to cheat, which isn't the best impression to make. Not every writer out there can afford the best screenwriting software, so always be conservative when making comments, and be aware that some software uses a layout that writers can't adjust, so it might not be something that they have any control over.

If poor formatting is happening frequently enough that it becomes cumbersome, such as including unnecessary empty lines on the page, having additional blank pages in the .pdf, using dual dialogue when characters are clearly not talking at the same time etc., then advise the writer gets to grips with the expected industry layout by reading more screenplays, using screenplay software, or possibly employing an editor to help whip the script into shape.

> **CHEATS**
>
> Consider adjusting the page margins to match the industry standard in order to ensure that the page count is an accurate representation of the script length.
>
> Any professional reader will instantly know that the page margins and the formatting is slightly off, so consider investing in some screenwriting software to help combat this, or at least double-check the format against the industry-standard layout.

ALTERING THE PAGE COUNT WILL ADD DESIRABILITY

This applies to all formats, but it's more common to find this issue with short scripts. Technically, a short film can be anything up to forty-minutes long, but declining attention spans and easily consumable online content mean that film festivals are increasingly opting for shorter films. Not only does this allow them to fit more films into a program, certain festivals only accept specific film lengths, so a writer might want to carefully consider whether their script is going to suit the film festivals that can best promote their work. If you're reading a short script that's over 15-pages long it's worth pointing out the limitations that comes with this.

A screenplay that's horrendously long or is very text-heavy not only indicates that the script is going to be a slow and laborious read, it shows that the writer can't contain story. That 90-120-page rule is there for a reason. It's to show that a writer has discipline and can work within limitations. This is even more essential for TV writers where tight time-slots and commercial breaks must be adhered to. There's almost always scope to make a script leaner by cutting back on the word count by doing a harsh edit, which will ultimately make the script leaner and more effective. If that's not an option, suggest that the content be broken into two separate movies/the next episode instead.

On the flip side of the coin, a shorter than average feature script can be a sign that the writer ran out of ideas and that the story is probably going to be lacking, in which case advise the writer focus on adding some new sub-plots or fleshing out existing ones. Are there any scenes what lack conflict and need more added? Does there need to be a quiet moment of reflection inserted in between the action? Are story beats happening too quickly? Is there any moment where something is clearly lacking etc.?

> **CHEATS**
>
> With short films, often it's the shorter, the better. Film festivals may choose a shorter film over a longer one, simply because it means they can fit more movies into a program. Cutting this piece down to 10-15 pages could increase its chances of getting picked up.
>
> While there is an epic story here, be aware that producers/execs are less likely to take a big financial risk on a new writer or a writer that's not able to contain their story to the industry standard 90-120 pages. Shortening the page count will help to cut the budget and make the script more appealing, so it's worth executing a harsh edit in order to give the script the best chance possible.
>
> Writers trying to break into TV writing need to demonstrate that they can contain story to a specific page limit. Do more research. Know who this piece will be pitched to and know what length of script they're going to expect.

MARKETABILITY

Most spec scripts that contest or coverage service readers read are usually going to be written by relatively new writers trying to get their first break, so the more marketable and appealing their script is, the more chance they have of kick-starting their career. It's a lot easier to then go off and break the rules after you've made it rather than to try and get funding for an obscure movie, especially if the writer doesn't have a lot of experience, so convincing writer's to play things by the book is very much in their own interests at this early stage.

Consider making a comment if;

IT ONLY HAS NICHE APPEAL

Niche can be good. In fact, it can be great, as there's often less competition and there is a dedicated, but small, audience waiting for new content, but it's also going to make a script a lot harder to sell. That doesn't mean it's not possible. There are lots of successful projects that took an extra-long time to come to fruition. *The Queen's Gambit* (2020) took 30 years to transform from book to miniseries, mostly because no one thought a TV show about chess would make any money, but hey, it did and was very successful.

It's not your job to discourage the writer from writing a passion project, and nor should you. You can only point out that the project has limited appeal and that the script may be difficult to sell. This either means that the writer needs to do more work on making the script a lot more marketable by giving it some universal appeal, or they should focus on finding producers or execs who will share their passion for the subject in the hopes of selling it with little change.

CHEATS

While there's certainly value in targeting a niche audience, consider whether there's scope to widen the scripts appeal so as not to limit its potential to sell.

This script makes a great portfolio piece that has the potential to do well in contests, which can certainly open doors, but with limited market appeal, be aware that this could be a difficult piece to sell.

Be aware that some producers/execs/studios may not be drawn to the piece because of its limited audience appeal. Either consider making the premise less niche in order to attract a wider audience, or target potential buyers with a history of producing similar projects.

IT WON'T APPEAL TO ITS TARGET AUDIENCE

If a writer has a Disney-type animation that's aimed at younger viewers but the script contains some strong language and has a few scenes that are of an adult nature, then they've slightly missed the mark when trying to appeal to their target audience. Similarly, if you're reading an adaptation of a popular contemporary novel but the script doesn't include the fans' favorite secondary character, then the movie probably isn't going to please the people it hopes will be its guaranteed audience.

Either the writer needs to alter their script to better please the people most likely to watch it, or they need to consider making changes to fit a different target audience altogether. In both instances, encourage the writer to keep the scripts intended audience in mind when writing. What does the writer want them to be feeling during every scene? What expectations will the viewers have? Should the writer bend to them or break away and create an unexpected twist? And is the content of the script going to please or put off its prospective viewers?

CHEATS
Try to keep the target audience in mind when writing. Understanding what material will be suitable for them and which won't will help to avoid mistakes such as (examples from the script).
This piece has the potential to appeal to two very different target audiences, but this means that the content that appeals to one may not necessarily appeal to the other and vice versa. At this stage, it's perhaps worth committing the script to just one demographic to avoid leaving two separate ones feeling unfulfilled.
Understanding what the target audience desires and doesn't desire from a story will help ensure that enough is being done to satisfy those viewers as well as avoid the moments they may find off-putting. Take (scene from the script) for example, will (genre) fans appreciate this break away from the norm, or does it risk ruining the experience for them?

IT'S TRYING TO PLEASE TOO MANY PEOPLE

A script that can successfully pull off having a little bit of everything is hard to find. More often than not, a newbie writer will attempt to write a story that appeals to as wide an audience as possible, cramming in too many genres and tropes in the hope that it'll maximize its profit and its chances of selling. Unfortunately, in these instances, the writer ends up pleasing no one, as they've spread all the different genres too thin. In such cases, you'll need to point out the consequences of not committing strongly to one or two genres.

Take a political drama set in the 14th century with a few magical elements and a couple of sword fights, for example. This has the potential to appeal to period fans, fantasy fans, and action buffs, but without the right balance, the period fans might be put off by inaccurate and illogical magic, the fantasy fans could be put off by the political drama featuring more than the magic, and the action fans will be left disappointed with only a handful of action scenes throughout.

Advise the writer to consider who their movie is really aimed at and to ask themselves if their script is going to fulfill that demographic's expectations or not. Genre categories exist for a reason; to make a movie more marketable, and while it's not uncommon to see movies classed as anywhere up to four different genres now, if those films were successful, it was because they got the balance right.

CHEATS

There are elements of (list the separate genres in the script) coming through in this script, but in trying to appeal to as many viewers as possible, there's the risk that none will be satisfied in the end. Consider tailoring the story more towards a specific target audience rather than to everyone to ensure that no one is left feeling disappointed.

With too many genre elements, tropes, and motifs occurring throughout the story, by trying to appeal to a broad audience, the movie has actually become harder to market. Genres exist for a reason and that's to sell movies. Take more time to figure out which specific audience this piece would appeal to the most and consider targeting the content towards satisfying them. By trying to please too many people, there's the risk that none end up being pleased in the process.

IT LACKS INTERNATIONAL APPEAL

Not every script needs to have international appeal, so this comment is more aimed towards writers who are trying to break into a foreign film market. If you've got a writer based in India who's written a Bollywood story, for example, but is hoping to sell it in the Hollywood market, there's probably going to be lots of elements in that script that won't appeal to western audiences. The writer either needs to adapt their script to suit the market they want to sell in, or consider finding a home-grown audience first.

If you have a writer who has written an exciting high-concept drama but it's set in Outer Mongolia, you'd need to ask whether the hard-to-reach and expensive shooting location is pivotal to the plot, or whether the story could be easily set in a less-expensive location without taking too much away from the story? Propose two options to the writer here. Either they need to make the location absolutely pivotal to the story so that it couldn't be set anywhere else, highlighting cultural elements, opening the viewer's eyes to a new world, and increasing the chances of finding funding (this depends on whether the county has a film fund body, but there's also plenty of funding available for international projects out there too), or the writer needs to consider changing the location (and possibly the nationality of the characters) to suit whichever market they want to appeal to, making the piece more recognizably relatable to the viewers, and lessening the budget in order to appeal to more producers. Think of it as having to justify the added expense of using an unusual location or setting.

CHEATS

Setting the story in a difficult-to-shoot location, such as (wherever the story is set), could limit the interest in this script for several reasons, but increasing the budget is likely to be at the very top. Either consider changing the setting to something more manageable, or alter the story so that it absolutely couldn't be set anywhere else This could open up the project to international collaboration possibilities, which often come with additional financial support.

At present, there's a universally themed story with plenty of appeal here, but technically, there's nothing preventing this story from being set elsewhere in the world. This is great as it means you can quickly make adaptations to suit a producer or execs notes, but is it also worth doing more to root the story in (the current location), meaning that it couldn't possibly take place anywhere else? This is certainly something to consider, especially if there are funding schemes based in (current location) who look for projects that bring positive attention to the area as any secured funding helps to make a script more appealing.

THERE'S A LACK OF DIVERSITY

Hollywood is increasingly calling out for more inclusive and diverse scripts, and rightly so, but this doesn't necessarily mean that writers should feel pressured into writing about communities, groups, or subject matters they don't have a lot of personal experience in. It's probably not a great idea for someone to write a piece about the challenges of being disabled without having a great deal of knowledge and understanding on the subject first, for example. The same applies to writing characters from different cultural backgrounds where there's the risk that portrayals may become stereotypical and unrealistic. And not every single story would benefit from being more diverse, so a judgement call has to be made. A historical drama about building Stonehenge wouldn't exactly be very factually accurate if it contained a very ethnically diverse cast. That's not to say it can't be done of course.

With that in mind, scripts, more often than not, are still forgetting to better reflect the diverse audiences they have the ability to harness. Viewers want to emotionally connect to a piece, and having characters they can relate to helps achieve this. Adding diversity to a script can add more layers to the conflict, the believability, and widen the audience appeal too. Plus, it's a great way to ensure that every character in a script feels unique and memorable. Increasing diversity doesn't mean adding in a token colored character. There are all sorts of different ways to add variety to what otherwise might be a rather uniform, restricted, or unimaginative story, such as including varying genders, sexualities, age groups, cultural backgrounds, disabilities, or limitations. Encourage writers to see increasing diversity in their scripts as another way to make it more standout, creative, and unique, rather than it being a forced rule that they have to adhere to.

CHEATS

Could adding more diversity into the cast also help create more mini-conflicts in the story, which would help flesh it out even further? Would coming from another culture, having a challenging disability/limitation, be struggling with gender or sexuality, etc., bring new conflicts, problems, or tests for the characters to face?

> **CHEATS CONT.**
>
> Does the script possibly need to show a more accurate representation of contemporary life? At present, the cast is fairly typical, but that also risks them being rather bland too. It's not about adding diversity just for the sake of it here, but consider what new challenges and conflicts could be created by including multi-layered characters who are also battling all too familiar prejudices that the audience can relate to.

BELIEVABILITY

Technically, every movie is set in a fictional world, but even if the story is set in the most unbelievable fantasy world, it still needs to have an element of believability in order for the audience to connect with it, and this is done by establishing rules in the story world. Having a character suddenly have the ability to fly isn't going to be taken seriously by the audience unless they're given some sort of explanation or 'rule' to rationalize it, such as 'everyone can fly when they come of age' or 'the character didn't realize the shoes they stole were gravity defying'.

Verisimilitude gives a movie the appearance of being realistic, with details, characters, and subjects that feel similar to real life. Characters need to be plausible and viewers need to believe that the words they say and the actions they take are credible. If story world rules are established and then broken, this too risks adding an unnecessary element of unbelievability to a script and any time a reader has to stop in order to question logic, the spell has been broken and they're no longer immersed in the story world. And if a reader is questioning something in the plot, you'd better believe the audience will do the same while watching too.

Consider making a comment if;

CHARACTERS MAKE IMPLAUSIBLE DECISIONS

We're not talking about characters making illogical actions or reactions here, such as going down into a dark cellar at night to investigate a strange noise all alone after having had a seance there the night before, we're talking about unbelievable decisions that would cause the audience to say "that would never happen in real life", like being caught totally unaware that your brother might re-animate after being bitten by a zombie-like creature. Culturally, it's common knowledge that an infected victim can turn, so it would be hard to believe a character who didn't know this in a movie. Similarly, an audience probably wouldn't swallow an E.R. doctor who has no medical knowledge whatsoever or that a ten-year-old schoolboy decides to take on five highly trained paratroopers (and wins) with no explanation. Without credible reason, these things wouldn't be believable.

If characters are making bizarre decisions, the writer needs to do more to explain the motivation behind the action in order to avoid completely puzzling the audience. There needs to be a driving motivation behind every action taken, so if a devoted father who is desperately trying to save his daughter from terrorists for the majority of the script is given an ultimatum at the end; his daughter's life or the life of the female cop who's helping him, and he saves the cop, will the audience believe it, and more importantly, will they be satisfied by that ending?

Highlight that without some sort of explanation being given, the writer may risk alienating their audience when a character takes an irrational action. Use specific examples from the script and ask questions. What's motivating the character to do this? How likely will the audience accept this without explanation? Do you need to do more to reveal the driving force behind this action, etc.?

CHEATS

In order to retain believability, every action that the characters make, no matter how stupid, has to be plausible, but audiences may struggle to understand why (character) suddenly decides to (action from the script) without some sort of explanation that justifies this.

It's worth giving the audience some insight into what's motivating (character) during the script. When (character) does (irrational action), it's difficult to understand what's driving this action, and it almost feels out of character, so consider adding something to help explain this, otherwise, there's the risk that the audience might not swallow it.

> **CHEATS CONT.**
>
> As this isn't a comedy script, so be careful not to go overboard with the farcical moments that risk it becoming one. When (character) suddenly (irrational action from the script), it creates a 'that would never happen in real life' moment for the viewers because it seems so implausible. Either do more to explain (how this was possible/what motivated the character to do this/why this happened, etc.) or work on making that action more credible so that the audience will have no problem believing it.

THERE ARE NOTICEABLE PLOT HOLES

Some plot holes are forgivable if they're small enough, but anything that sticks out like a sore thumb is likely to leave audiences feeling slightly unsatisfied after watching. A plot hole is any inconsistency in the story, any impossible moments that occur, factual errors, characters acting out of character, or contradictory events and statements, all of which can create confusion.

A plot hole can easily be the result of restructuring during a previous rewrite or perhaps the writer still very much has the story in their mind as opposed to down on the page, meaning that there may be some pivotal details that haven't been expressed yet. Thankfully, the writer has you on hand to point out any glaringly obvious discrepancies.

Encourage writers to figure out what information is missing and what they can insert into the plot in order to fill the hole. It could be a case of adding more setup that helps to explain the scenario. If it's a character-driven plot hole, again, mention that the audience may need to further understand what's motivating the character to take such an unexpected action. And if it's incorrect factual information being given, indicate that the writer may need to do a little more research on the subject. There's nothing worse than discovering your script has a glaringly obvious plot hole after you've written it, so be gentle.

> **CHEATS**
>
> A little more research might be needed on (subject matter) in order to make the piece more credible. There are a few instances, such as (examples from the script) that stand out as being obvious inaccuracies. Finding an expert who's willing to look over the script could be an excellent way to find any other instances as well as giving other useful insight into that (world/era/industry, etc.) that could also be integrated.
>
> It's easy to lose track of the plot during the early drafts, but a couple of glaringly obvious plot holes that need to be filled are (examples from the script). Figuring out what led up to those moments, as well as where they lead to next, will help achieve this.
>
> Don't forget to tie up all the small loose ends just as much as with the central plot. There are a few unanswered questions, such as (what happens to?/where did … disappear to?/does … ever get resolved?, etc.) that an audience will want to be answered. Do a pass ensuring that every character or plot point that needs a conclusion gets one.

BUDGET

Writers don't necessarily have to keep budget in mind when writing a spec script, in fact, there probably shouldn't be any limits placed on their imagination at such an early stage, but a producer or exec is less likely to risk wagering an excessively high budget on a new writer who is yet to sell anything or on someone who is yet to prove their worth. Big budget movies also mean that a script needs to be in near perfect condition, as every added cost needs to be justified. On the other side of the coin, well-written low budget movies, especially in certain genres, such as comedy, rom-com, or horror, have the potential to reap high rewards with lower risk, which gives them a greater chance of selling.

Consider making a comment if;

THERE ARE TOO MANY CHARACTERS

The bigger the cast, the bigger the budget needs to be. Even more so if there are lots of minor characters with speaking lines. It's also not great practice when writing a spec script as readers don't enjoy having dozens of character names to remember and there's the risk that some will be forgotten or will blend in with other characters.

Often, scenes become longer than they need to be because a writer has minor characters interrupting the action or drama with small pieces of dialogue, such as a waiter taking an order, an unnamed soldier acknowledging a command, or a snarky receptionist delaying a meeting. Longer shooting times need larger budgets, and speaking parts cost more than non-speaking parts. If dialogue from a minor character is interrupting the dramatic momentum of a scene, advise the writer considers removing the character, or their dialogue, and try to convey the same message using visuals instead.

Detailing who is present during each scene also takes up extra space on the page, so if you've got five or six individuals present but only three of them are talking, the other three should at least be doing something that's also moving the plot forward or it begs the question whether they need to be present at all. Ask the writer to examine what purpose or role each minor character is performing and to consider whether they're absolutely needed. Could two or three characters be amalgamated into a single character in order to help cut the budget? Could a line be delivered by a more prominent character instead? Is having too many characters pulling focus away from the main plot, etc.?

CHEATS

This is a cast-heavy script and not only does that take up a lot of scene description space when they each appear on screen, it's also difficult to keep track of every character too. In addition, the more line-speaking characters there are, the bigger the budget needs to be. Consider trimming back on the number of minor characters needed to tell this story.

> **CHEATS CONT.**
>
> Make the story more digestible and easier to follow by cutting back on the large number of characters used. Look for any characters who could be amalgamated into just the one, any characters that aren't serving a pivotal purpose to the story, or any minor characters that could play non-speaking roles instead. This will help to make the script feel less cluttered and it'll also help cut the budget required too.

THERE ARE TOO MANY LOCATIONS

This isn't going to be a major talking point when writing coverage for new writers, but if you're giving feedback on a short film, or a script that's already got funding and working within a certain budget constraint, then it's worth pointing out cost-saving suggestions that won't harm the overall story.

Changing the shooting location during production adds to the budget as everything, from cast, crew, equipment, and catering, has to be transported elsewhere. This primarily applies to external locations, as anything that's shot in a studio is pretty much self-contained and a lot cheaper too. Altering the location can help keep a piece visually engaging, so it's understandable why writers would want to avoid scenes taking place in the same old place too often, but if action is occurring in a brand new location to no real advantage, it's worth suggesting the writer considers reusing previous locations in order to minimize the cost.

Montages can also often turn into overly expensive sequences if they're using multiple shots from around the world, showing different weather systems, or contain large crowds of people etc., so you'll need to assess the overall effectiveness of the montage first in order to determine whether it's something that's adding anything to the story or is a potential cut.

> **CHEATS**
>
> This indie script has an excellent chance of getting produced. Help increase that chance even further by making sure that every change in location is absolutely necessary. Every little helps when it comes to minimizing the budget, so if there's a way to cut down the number of locations, especially external ones, it's worth examining.
>
> To cut down the page count or minimize the budget required in order to give the script more appeal to independent producers, look for any scenes that could be condensed into just one location, consider placing external scenes internally, and try to use locations more than once.

THE WRITER SITES COPYRIGHTED MATERIAL

This is another mistake that risks giving off an amateur vibe and you'll commonly see a writer list a specific song title during the first act and it'll become a reoccurring feature throughout the rest of the script. Not only is dictating the soundtrack someone else's job, unless a writer has obtained the rights to use the material themselves, there's no guarantee that the budget will be big enough to do this, or that the owner of the material will allow its use.

Unless a song, movie, or television clip is absolutely pivotal to the plot, it's just needless decoration that's taking up space on the page, especially if it's a track that the reader has never heard of, and therefore doesn't have any actual impact. Encourage the writer to add `in the vein of` or be more general in their description, such as `an upbeat pop track plays on the radio of the wrecked car`, or `a classic slasher horror movie plays on the TV in the background` to allow for flexibility when finding material that fits.

> **CHEATS**
>
> Be aware that any music tracks mentioned in the script are likely to be removed due to copyright issues. Unless the rights have been purchased, consider adding "in the vein of" to suggest that type of music instead.

CHEATS CONT.

Listing music tracks only really works if the person reading the script knows the song. If they don't, it's just wasting space on the page. A good workaround is to suggest the genre and tone of the music instead, such as (reader's suggestion), so that the mood of the scene is being evoked without being overly specific.

The music tracks listed in the script don't feel pivotal to the plot, meaning that a similar track in the same vein could probably create the same effect. Avoid any copyright issues by suggesting the genre of music instead of a specific track, or better still, leave the soundtrack decisions up to the director.

STRUCTURE

Being familiar with the various act structures, the sequence approach, beat sheet breakdowns, key turning points, and deep scene structure is a must here. How a story is structured and the flow of dramatic momentum that's created will determine how an audience reacts to it. Placing a reveal at the beginning of the story, for example, will create a different reaction from the audience than it would if it was placed at the turn into the third act, so understanding narrative structure, how to effectively use narrative devices, and how to weave plot threads in relation to the emotion that a writer is trying to elicit is important.

As usual, begin with the positives. Did the story unfold naturally? How efficiently was the premise delivered? Was there a satisfactory conclusion? Was the story consistently engaging? Were there enough twists and turns to keep you on your toes throughout, etc.?

CHEATS

Another core strength is the structure, with well-paced acts, clear turning points on the page, and compelling dramatic momentum that consistently propels the story forward.

Moving locations works really well to visually indicate sequences and act breaks for the audience.

Story beats and turning points are not only clear on the page, showing that the piece is well-developed, there are clear A, B & C story threads, all of which have been allocated a suitable amount of screen time, revealing the writer's experience.

There's a quick setup to this story that efficiently establishes just who this story is about, what problem they face, what's getting in their way, and more importantly, why the audience should care.

There's a satisfying conclusion to this story that neatly wraps up every story thread, completes (the MC's) character arc, and there's a memorable twist that will create buzz for the audience too.

OPENING SEQUENCES

More often than not, many of the problems that become apparent during the body of a script can be traced back to issues with a poorly constructed opening. The first act is where a writer needs to establish who their story is about, what major problem they face, what big obstacle stands in their way, and why it's important that they succeed, but more importantly, why the audience should care. If just one of these questions isn't being answered during Act I, the writer isn't doing enough to hook the viewer, and that risks their screenplay not going any further either.

Consider making a comment if;

THERE'S NO HOOK

There are lots of commentaries about how many pages an agent, an exec, or more likely, their assistant, will give a screenplay before deciding to pass or continue reading. In reality, if an assistant's been tasked with assessing a piece of material, they'll more than likely be required to read the entire script, but essentially what every reader is looking for when starting a new script, is a great hook that propels them to keep turning the page.

Page-one is where the writer creates their first impression, and although it's not always possible, the quicker that gripping hook occurs, the better. A hook can be several things; a unique character, an unusual setting, an interesting question being posed, or immediate peril, etc., but some scripts begin as slow-burners, which is fine, as certain plots need a certain amount of setup before they get going, in which case, the writer needs to use their distinct writing voice to hook the reader and to keep them engrossed until the conflict begins.

If a script is lacking a hook early on, ask the writer to move things structurally so that they reach whatever hook there is much faster, to heighten the central problem that's occurring in order to make it more interesting or urgent, to create a character introduction that immediately makes us want to follow the MC, to create a memorable opening image, or to ensure that their writing style is compelling, enticing the reader to read on.

> **CHEATS**
>
> It's becoming increasingly essential to hook the reader from the very first page, and while there are (positive remarks about the script), there's also (negative remarks about the script). Consider (cutting back on the setup/evoking the tone much stronger/creating a moment of intrigue, etc.) as quickly as possible in order to give the reader a great reason to continue turning the page.
>
> There's a great inciting incident that creates (intrigue/interest/a page-turning moment, etc.), but unfortunately, the pages leading up to that moment aren't working as hard to grab the reader, and this risks them giving up before they get to that crucial moment. Either do more to enhance the writing, making it as compelling as possible, or trim down the amount of setup so that we get to the inciting incident much sooner.
>
> While the overall premise is a good one, there's not a lot to hook the reader on the first few pages, where the all-important first impression is made. (suggestion that will help make the first few pages more engaging) could help grab the reader and keep them turning the page, ensuring that they don't give up on the script too early.

THE MC ISN'T IN THE FIRST SCENE

Traditionally, movies usually open with a scene that introduces the lead character. This isn't an absolute rule by any means, but it works well to allow an audience to quickly understand who they're supposed to be following, and while there are plenty of exceptions to this, if a writer has opened with another character, there's the risk that it's giving a false expectation as to whom the protagonist actually is.

It may just be a case of re-arranging some early scenes, but make the writer aware that they may accidentally be giving the impression that a minor character is the focal point of the story if they've spent too much time establishing the setting, on world-building, or creating suspense instead of opening with the protagonist. An audience doesn't want to wait ten minutes to meet the hero of the movie or show.

> **CHEATS**
>
> Be aware that because (secondary character) is featured prominently during the first (scene/sequence), there's the risk that they're being established as the protagonist of the story, rather than (the MC).
>
> There's the risk of misleading the audience by choosing to open the story with a scene that has (secondary character) as the focus, rather than (the MC). Viewers will automatically assume that (secondary character) is who they're supposed to be following and invest in this character, making it feel awkward when it later becomes apparent that they've wasted that interest.

THERE'S TOO MUCH SETUP

This is a common feature in TV pilot episodes, where the writer has placed the inciting incident at the end of the episode in order to create a hook, meaning that the entire episode has just been an extended setup to deliver the series premise. In most cases, the audience needs to know what the premise of a show is from the first act, not the last one, or indeed, the next episode, but that's not to say it can't work in certain instances. If the episode is engaging before it delivers the premise, then there's probably enough to keep an audience entertained, but if in doubt, refer to the logline the writer has given or the one you construct yourself. If the inciting incident in the logline doesn't arrive until the last act of the show, then there's a potential problem.

This is also a common feature in biopics when the writer starts the story far too early, resulting in too much boring and unnecessary setup. We don't need to see a character literally be born in order to believe that they exist. Similarly, if there was no big character defining moment in a character's childhood, it's probably safe to say we don't need to see them growing up.

The same can of course apply to features and shorts. What they will all have in common is that nothing terribly interesting happens for an extended length of time. The inciting incident's supposed to hit around the 12-15-page mark in a feature (if not sooner), but don't get stuck adhering to recommended page numbers here. They're just a guide. It's more important to assess whether the writer is taking too long to get to the good stuff, in which case you need to tell them they risk the reader giving up before they have a chance to impress. Recommend that the writer minimize the setup and to re-evaluate when their story actually needs to begin.

> **CHEATS**
>
> It's becoming more and more essential to hit the ground running, hooking the reader straight away, unfortunately, this makes any slow-burning spec script slightly harder to sell. Minimizing the amount of setup is one way to combat this by jumping straight into the story as soon as possible.
>
> At present, it feels like it's taking that little bit too long for the good stuff to begin, and this risks a reader giving up and putting the script down too early, which should be avoided at all costs. Severely cutting the setup needed to get to the inciting incident, or possibly even starting with the inciting incident straight away then filling in the necessary details later on could help avoid this.
>
> Essentially, the end hook is really the inciting incident that establishes what the premise is for the viewers, meaning that the entire pilot is a long-winded setup to get to that point. The audience shouldn't have to wait until the end of the episode to discover what the show is about. That's something that they need to know from the first act. Could the second episode possibly make for a better pilot here?

SETUPS & PAYOFFS

Readers and audiences love setups and payoffs. They act as small rewards for having paid attention, and they also make for a more polished piece of writing as it gives everything in a story meaning. But this form of foreshadowing requires planning, and writers at an early stage of their career may need some extra guidance on how to use one of the most useful tools at their disposal.

Consider making a comment if;

SETUPS AREN'T PAID OFF

A setup that doesn't get paid off could end up being seen as needless filler that can easily be cut from a script. If a piece of information, prop, or action has been used and then never gets mentioned again, not only has the writer missed the opportunity to create a rewarding payoff, if the audience is expecting to see a payoff but don't then get one, they'll be left disappointed. Just look at the TV series *Lost* (2004-10) as an example. There were so many different clues, questions, and reveals dropped during the show that never came into fruition or led anywhere. When the series eventually ended, there was a whole host of unanswered questions left hanging that was very bittersweet for the audience.

Setups are easy to spot when reading, but if the writer is inexperienced, they may be over-describing details that may lead you to believe that they're a potential setup when, in fact, it's just an over-eager writer. Jot down potential setups as you take notes so that you can double check whether they got paid off. If they didn't, then you'll need to question the writer why they went out of their way to highlight certain props, had characters say certain lines, or included certain visuals. If they don't serve a function, they're wasting space on the page, so ask whether they could be cut or paid off in order to justify their inclusion.

CHEATS

Make sure that every setup gets paid off during the script. If there is no payoff, that makes any setup a potential cut, as it's not being as effective as it could be.

There are a couple of instances where attention is drawn to (examples of possible setups from the script), indicating that these are setups to later be paid off in the story, but unfortunately, none of these things are ever mentioned again. Either reuse these elements again by turning them into setups and payoffs, or consider cutting these otherwise space-filling pieces of information if they're not particularly pivotal to the plot.

Readers and audiences love setups and payoffs. They're like mini rewards for having paid attention and they're also great at displaying a writer's skill with story structure. Any lines, props, or actions that have been drawn attention to in the script could be used to foreshadow something further down the line, so it's worth doing a pass looking to make sure that every potential setup that's been created gets paid off.

Structure | 75

PAYOFFS AREN'T SETUP PROPERLY

If a payoff hasn't been foreshadowed enough, it can often come across as contrived, convenient, or too much of a coincidence. Take Captain Boomerang and the stuffed toy unicorn incident from *The Suicide Squad* (2021). We see this character hide a random unicorn toy inside the left side of his jacket, not once, but twice, so when we later watch him take a knife to the left of his chest, we're all a bit surprised to discover his life's been saved by the knife wedging into a wad of cash, not the unicorn, which is never seen ever again. While it's more than likely something changed during filming or got left on the cutting room floor, this is a visual example of what to avoid in a screenplay. The payoff of the wad of cash wasn't set up properly, and if this occurred in the script, the reader would have been left wondering where it came from, bringing them out of the story to question the logic.

If a payoff doesn't get the setup it needs, point out the plot hole to the writer at the same time as reminding them to avoid any instances where immersion into the story world breaks for the reader due to a confusing piece of exposition.

CHEATS

Double-check to make sure that all the payoffs have been properly set up to begin with. When (example from the script) occurs, it almost feels like it's come out of nowhere because there was no previous foreshadowing that this was going to happen. Avoid this moment feeling like a contrived coincidence that risks stretching the believability by adding a setup to explain it.

It's worth figuring out a way to better setup (example from the script), as at present, there's the risk that this event feels like a very convenient and easy fix to solve (the problem), and audiences may be left feeling cheated. Insert a moment that foreshadows this event so that it doesn't come as such as surprise when it happens.

SETUPS ARE TOO OBVIOUS

Revealing too much early on can quell any build-up of surprise, so understanding the balance between mystery and revelation is important here. If a setup is too obvious, it can create a predictable story, which should be avoided at all costs. Predictable means boring. If the audience feels like they know what's going to happen, on one-hand this can create anticipation, but on the other, there's the risk that they'll lose interest.

If there's a setup in a script that gets paid off exactly as you expected, spoiling the surprise, it's worth pointing this out to the writer with the advice that they do more to disguise the setup, make it more subtle, throw in a red herring, or to come up with a more unexpected payoff instead.

> **CHEATS**
>
> It's not going to come as any surprise to anyone when (obvious plot point from the script) occurs, because it was clearly foreshadowed back when (obvious setup) happened. Give that moment more shocking emotional impact for the viewers by making the setup much more subtle if possible.
>
> Do more to make certain moments less predictable. When viewers can clearly see what's going to happen, it lessens the excitement and it can lead to a boring plot. The viewers are going to expect (character) to (take specific action), (add more examples if necessary), so either play with these expectations by delivering something completely unexpected or don't make the setups to these events as obvious as they currently are.

STORY BEATS

A screenplay comprises of lots of story beats strung together, but what exactly is a story beat? Whether you're referring to Blake Snyder's beat sheet, the hero's journey, or something in between, a beat is a moment of change that moves the story forward. This can be an event, an interaction, a realization, or a resolution. They're a great tool to map out character arcs, story pace, and the emotional rollercoaster you want to take the audience on, but when story beats are missing or aren't particularly strong, it can lead to problems in these areas too.

Consider making a comment if;

THE PREMISE IS UNCLEAR DURING THE FIRST ACT

Another common issue, especially in TV pilots, is that the overall premise isn't clear enough. Ideally, by the end of the first act both the reader and the audience should understand who the story is about, why we should care enough about them to want to follow their story, what major problem they have, what's standing in the way of them solving it, and what they stand to lose if they cannot accomplish their goal. If you can't answer these questions by at least 15-pages into the script, then there's either too much setup setting happening, the writer isn't focusing enough on the protagonist, they may be trying to cram in too many story threads, or they've used a cold-open that doesn't feel connected to the main plot.

If there's more than one plot thread occurring, ask the reader to consider which one is going to be the most interesting for the audience and whether the secondary thread could possibly be distracting them from the story line they really want to follow? It's often better to use the opening act to firmly engross the viewers into the main story rather than barrage them with too many plot threads and characters all at the same time.

If this is happening in a feature script, remind the writer that if the plot isn't clear at the start of the story, a reader's going to quickly assume that the rest of the script will be just as confusing. That's not the best first impression to create, so advise they do more to make sure all of the above requirements are being met.

> **CHEATS**
>
> It's extremely important that the reader (and audience) can identify the premise during the first act, but here, it's not until (moment premise is established in the script) on page (No.) that it becomes clear what this story is about. Cut the amount of setup to help get to this moment faster. If a reader can't figure out what the story is during the first 30-40-pages, there's the risk that they'll stop reading altogether.

> **CHEATS CONT.**
>
> By the end of Act I, we need to know who the story is about, what big problem they face, who or what is standing in their way, and why we should care. While (character/goal/stakes/problem, etc.) has been clearly established, what's missing are the (antagonistic force/goal/stakes/problems, etc.), so do more work to ensure that the premise of the piece is much clearer during the early pages of the script.
>
> Arguably, because we have to wait right up until (event which establishes the premise) during the last act for the premise to be made clear, everything up until that point could be viewed as an extended setup sequence. This is the moment when the story essentially kicks off, so is it worth using this as the inciting incident, rather than the end of episode hook?

TURNING POINTS AREN'T CLEAR ON THE PAGE

Turing points and story beats signify a key change in the dramatic tone. They're the moments that change the direction of the story, propel it forward, increase the stakes, create questions or reveals. They're the inciting incidents, the break into Act II, the midpoint etc., and ideally, they should all be emotionally charged, exciting, and memorable moments (that usually feature the protagonist) and are clear on the page when reading the script. If they're not, then the writer's probably going to have a forgettable plot that's missing any increasing dramatic momentum.

Hooking the reader at the beginning is just the first step of many, as it's really something writers need to do continuously throughout a script. If there's nothing happening on the page to keep the reader interested, there's not a lot compelling them to keep turning the page, and that's something writers need to remember. If it's hard to pinpoint the major story beats when writing the synopsis, you'll know that the writer hasn't done enough, so recommend that they refer to their beat sheet, if they have one (or to write out a new one), and to find a way of heightening the conflict or emotion further. Perhaps the protagonist is a missing feature or needs to be more active during those scenes. A lack of high stakes could also lead to weak turning points, so if you can see the root of the problem, highlight it to the writer.

> **CHEATS**
>
> Some beats are stronger than others on the page, so it's worth taking a second look at the major turning points in the script, which should all focus on the protagonist and be heightened emotional moments that are memorable.
>
> While there are some really strong story beats occurring, such as (example from the script), others feel fairly flat and are easily missed, such as (the break into Act II/midpoint/ focal point 2, etc.) where there's a lack of (heightened emotion/drama/gripping conflict, etc.).
>
> Not every story beat is as clear as it could be on the page. Go back to the beat sheet here in order to pinpoint those all-important turning points. These are the memorable, emotionally charged instances of heightened drama that keep the viewers engaged throughout the story, but at present, they're not quite packing the powerful punch they have the potential to create.

THERE'S A WEAK POINT OF NO RETURN

The midpoint is one of the easier beats to spot as it usually has a clear purpose, but that's not to say it always has to signify the moment in the protagonist's journey where they've no choice but to forge forward as the option to turn back has been removed. The midpoint can also create a false victory or a false fail for the MC too, but it all comes down to whether the story shifts up a gear or not. As with any turning point or beat, things have to be interesting, and if that's lacking at midpoint, there's going to be a lot of mediocre on either side, meaning there's very likely a long time in the script that lacks plot, lacks conflict, and lacks any hooks.

If the midpoint is clearly lacking, advise the writer to go back and really make sure they nail this beat. While no one really leaves the cinema raving about the midpoint of a movie, in screenwriting terms, it can signify that the writer has run out of steam and the story is just going through the motions until it reaches the end climax. Remind the writer that if the reader's attention is beginning to flag during the middle of the script, so will the audiences.

> **CHEATS**
>
> Would adding a strong moment of no return for (protagonist) help to strengthen this character's arc? Introducing an instance where it's now impossible for them to turn back and metaphorically go home, meaning that they have no choice but to forge forward could help to add some much-needed tension, drama, and urgency to the plot.
>
> There's the sense that the conflict begins to run out of steam as the story (approaches/passes) midpoint, meaning this beat needs to be much stronger than it currently is.
>
> The change in location at midpoint creates a great visual indicator that tells the audience that the story is now moving in a new direction, but when reaching (new location), there's not a lot of new (conflict/exposition/reveals/twists/emotionally charged moments, etc.) happening, which lessens the impact this midpoint moment should have.

THE END HOOK IS WEAK

If you're reading a pilot episode, the writer may have attempted to end on a big hook to help entice viewers back for the next episode. From a selling point of view, having a gripping hook will almost always be preferable to not having one, but they aren't always needed, and many great shows don't use the device, so this isn't something that you should demand a writer has in their script. You can, however, point out the advantages, such as how a great hook makes an excellent talking point for the audience, how it invites them to want to carry on watching, and that they're also great at helping the following episode get straight into the action with minimal setup needed. A weak hook, however, doesn't do any of these things and can create an anti-climax instead.

An end hook can be anything from creating a big new question that we want answered, a surprise reveal, an unexpected reversal, or a character put into peril, etc. If the script comes under the expected page count, then there's no real harm in encouraging the writer to add a hook, but the emphasis usually needs to be on the protagonist here. Too often, a writer will create a hook for a secondary character, which isn't as enticing as it would be if they created the problem for the MC instead. If an end hook is too vague, cryptic, or easily misunderstood, it's missing out on maximizing its impact, so if there is a weak hook, try to explain to the writer why.

Obviously, this can also occur in feature scripts where the writer wants to set up a sequel, and while this can work well to show that the movie has potential to become a franchise, it's a risk, especially if the main plot doesn't have a satisfactory conclusion and the writer is relying on interest in a second script to answer some of the plot questions created in the first.

> **CHEATS**
>
> While ending on (example from the script) is a great way to show that TV structure has very much been kept in mind while writing, this scene possibly creates more confusion than intrigue. Either do more to turn it into a more compelling "what happened next?" moment or consider saving this scene for the next episode.
>
> Consider cutting the tag scene, which doesn't have a particularly strong hook, and end on the more powerful (last act moment) instead, which is by far more memorable and engaging scene. Don't risk the weaker tag diminishing the impact of the end scene here.
>
> It's great that the writer believes there is enough material to write a sequel script, but consider omitting the end teaser from this spec. If the script garners attention, by all means, pitch it as the first of a possible franchise, but having a strong, memorable conclusion to the story being told in this script is going to be what impresses the reader more here.

SCENE STRUCTURE

You're more likely going to discuss this when dealing with well-developed screenplays than with first-time writers who are still mastering the basics. Understanding everything that a scene needs to have is essential here. Every scene has a beginning, middle, and end, and during that time the plot needs to have moved forward in some manner, meaning that a character should either be closer or further from achieving their goal. This can be achieved by various means, such as through character, by revealing a new piece of information, or throwing in an obstacle and creating conflict, but the point is that each scene progresses the story and ideally leaves the reader wanting to keep turning the pages. In theory, this sounds simple enough to do. In practice, it's part of the rewriting progress where writers can easily become bogged down without direction.

Consider making a comment if;

THE PLOT HASN'T ADVANCED BY THE END OF THE SCENE

Any scene that doesn't advance the plot is a potential cut as they're stagnating the pace, the drama, and adding needless words for the reader to plow through. You'll quickly be able to identify scenes like this because they don't deliver any new information, there's no new obstacle or challenge being presented, and the protagonist is no further forward in their quest. Sometimes it feels like a writer has just written these space-filling scenes in order to bump up the page count when there wasn't enough sustainable plot to keep going.

It's easy for new writers to not realize that every scene needs to serve a purpose, so if you find any redundant scenes in a script, it's worth highlighting them to the writer. Advise that something needs to have changed during a scene, otherwise it's not being effective. Ask them to keep the MC's goal in mind during rewrites and to figure out a way to move them either closer or further away from that goal by the end of each scene. Simply adding in a new piece of pivotal information is an easy way to make a redundant scene become useful.

> **CHEATS**
>
> At times, the pace of the story flounders due to the story not moving forward during certain scenes. Take (example from the script), where (the MC) doesn't seem any further forward or any further away from achieving their goal, meaning that this stagnant scene is a potential cut.
>
> Do a pass to make sure at least one new piece of pivotal information is being delivered in each scene to ensure that there are no scenes that aren't moving the story forward. If no new info is being given, consider what the point of the scene actually is and whether it's adding anything to the story. This will help to increase the pace of both the plot and the read too.

Structure | 83

> **CHEATS CONT.**
>
> If the plot hasn't advanced by the end of a scene, it becomes a potential cut, so it's worth keeping this in mind during the next rewrite. Take (scene from the script) for example, where there's no crucial new piece of information being delivered, (the MC) has got no closer to or further from achieving their goal, and if anything, the scene is covering old ground that we already know. Either cut scenes like this or add something new to ensure that they're pivotal.

SCENES REPEAT NEEDLESS INFORMATION

Repeating info can be very useful, such as reminding the audience about what's at stake, showing the passage of time, hammering home a pivotal piece of information, or it can help add to the comedy when used as part of a running gag, but often when we come across information that we already know during a scene, it's down to sloppy writing and it risks insulting the audiences intelligence at the same time. A classic example would be the protagonist receiving information from one character in one scene, then delivering that same exact information to someone else in the next scene, forcing the audience to hear the same thing twice, which isn't just boring, it's wasting precious time too.

If a writer is guilty of spending too much time regurgitating the plot during the script, advise they do a pass trying to limit these instances and explain exactly why it'll benefit their script. Ask them to consider condensing scenes or find a new and interesting way of delivering the same exposition that adds something if they absolutely believe they need those scenes.

> **CHEATS**
>
> Be careful not to spend too much time repeating information that we already know. Take, (example from the script), which becomes a potential cut because (information already given), begging the question does this really need to be reiterated to the audience?

> **CHEATS CONT.**
>
> Repetition works well when it's used to hammer home a pivotal point or to remind the audience of something after a long period of time, but it's less effective when not enough time has passed or the exposition isn't particularly riveting. Telling us (example from the script) so soon after first disclosing it risks underestimating the audience's intelligence. Either include an additional pivotal piece of new information here or consider cutting the repetition altogether.
>
> Trim down the word count and increase the pace of both the story and the read by not repeating information unnecessarily. Take (example from the script), for instance, as we already know (information given), does it really need to be repeated here too? (use other examples from the script to further highlight the problem too).

SCENES HAVE NO CONFLICT

This isn't an absolute rule, so if there are scenes in a script that don't have a great deal of conflict but are still effectively pushing the story forward, revealing character, or are entertaining, you shouldn't be suggesting that a writer forces an element of conflict into them unnecessarily. If, however, you find scenes are boring, flat, and unengaging, there's every chance it's because there isn't enough conflict occurring.

It's not enough for a writer to save the conflict for the big turning points and story beats. They need to get into the habit of ensuring that there's conflict in as many scenes as possible. While there are countless ways to create conflict, both subtle and overt, a writer really needs to first understand what exactly their protagonist is trying to achieve in both their external goals and their inner emotional needs. If they know what their MC wants, then they can throw obstacles in the way, create complications, and keep the story rolling forward.

Advise the writer re-examine the scenes that lack conflict and ask them to figure out who wants what, why, and what's getting in the way of them achieving that for each of the characters present. Conflict doesn't always need to come from another character, of course. It can be environmental, technological, supernatural, inner-conflict, and societal conflict etc., but if the protagonist isn't facing any challenges, hard decisions, or problems, the writer's probably making things far too easy for them, and that's not going to satisfy audiences.

> **CHEATS**
>
> There are (a few/several/many, etc.) scenes where the conflict begins to drop, and that risks losing the audience's attention. Take (scene from the script) for example, where there's (not a lot of new information being delivered/characters are talking about things we already know/the story isn't moving forward, etc.). Upping the conflict would help combat this.
>
> Not every scene absolutely needs to contain conflict, but it's a key factor in keeping the audience engaged, so it's well worth making sure that as many scenes as possible contain some. Take (scene from the script) as an example. (give reasons why the current scene is flat/stagnant/forgettable, etc.). Look for ways to create additional conflict to keep things interesting for the viewers.
>
> With dramatic momentum in mind, watch out for scenes that don't contain enough conflict, which risk creating a dip in the rising tension that's being created at the wrong time. Take (example from the script), where there's (no real conflict occurring/the plot isn't moving forward/there's no interesting new information being delivered, etc.), which slows the pace at a time when it should be increasing.

SCENES ARE TOO LONG

More often than not, emerging writers will tend to have longer than necessary scenes. It differs from genre to genre, but in general, scenes shouldn't last any longer than three-pages. If they do, advise the writer does a pass using the 'enter late, leave early' rule. This means getting straight into the meat of a scene and ending it on the strongest visual or line possible. The more you read, the more you'll able to quickly spot when a scene should've ended, but the writer added in one or two unnecessary lines of dialogue that lessened the potential big punch that it had.

Greetings, goodbyes, entering and exiting can very often be cut without hindering the story. The audience doesn't need to see characters arrive or leave to understand how they got there or where they're going. Any other lines that aren't helping to move the story forward are also potential cuts.

Waffling dialogue is usually the culprit behind scenes being overly long, but over description of unnecessary props, actions, and boring scene setting in the scene description can also make a scene *feel* too long even if that doesn't equate to more pages of script.

As when trying to identify pacing issues, if your attention starts to wane during a scene, something's probably not working. If you deem it's because scenes are overly long, the writer needs to know. If there was a strong line or visual that the writer bypassed, get the writer to ask themselves which line they think will create the biggest impact on the viewers; the strong line/visual versus whatever the subsequent action or chit-chat dialogue that proceeded it? This is a great way to encourage the writer to keep the viewers' emotions in mind when writing. Similarly, if the scene takes too long to get to the meat, indicate that spending too much time setting up a scene risks interrupting the pace of the story and dampening any tension, drama, or suspense that had been created in the scenes beforehand.

CHEATS

The average scene length is (1-3-pages in a feature/1.5-2.5-pages in a TV pilot) and while this is just a rough guide, keeping the majority of scenes short and punchy like this helps to create good pace and keeps audiences engaged. At present, the average scene length in this script is much longer and often unnecessarily so, meaning that there's room to trim things down to help make the script leaner.

When scenes run too long, it becomes difficult to keep the audience continually engaged, so the shorter, the better. Apply the 'enter late, leave early' rule, which means minimizing the setup, jumping straight into the meat of the scene, before ending on the strongest line or visual possible.

Increase the pace of both the story and the read by shortening the scene length. The 'enter late, leave early' rule can really help here. Jump straight into the meat of a scene and then leave on a powerful note. Cut the unnecessary fluff such as greetings and goodbyes, any chit-chat dialogue, or unimportant scene description to keep scenes lean and to the point.

SUBPLOTS

Subplots aren't essential and not every story needs to include them. You won't often find any subplots in a short film, for example, as there simply isn't enough time to include them. If the protagonist is iconic enough to keep us gripped all the way through a script, then using subplots for the sake of using them would end up taking screen time away from the character the audience wants to stay focused on. TV shows, on the other hand, almost always include subplots (or rather, B-stories, which don't necessarily need to feature the protagonist) in order to keep the audience engaged and to ensure every cast member gets some time on screen.

What subplots are particularly good for, is providing some light-relief in between high-octane action sequences, expressing the central theme from another angle, enriching character development by revealing new information about the MC, or adding a love-story thread, but often subplots can be neglected, feel disconnected, and come across as space-filler if not done well.

Consider making a comment if;

THERE'S A DISTINCT LACK OF SUBPLOTS

When assessing television scripts, you need to determine whether the main story is strong enough to carry a full episode on its own or whether adding other storylines is required. The most common TV structure contains a primary A-story followed by a smaller B-story and an even smaller C-story, but some half-hour scripts may only contain two story threads rather than three.

When trying to assess this, ask whether the episode features interesting minor characters that are possibly being under-used and who deserve to have more screen time. Does the A-story dwindle and run out of steam at any point, which might be eased by including another thread to help keep the dramatic momentum going? Does the page count come significantly under the expected length, indicating there's enough room to insert a subplot? And is there scope to explore a variation of the central theme using secondary characters in their own subplot thread?

All of which apply when dealing with feature scripts too. Advise that a writer seriously considers adding in or fleshing out more subplots in order to add depth to the story, increase the conflict, explore theme, tighten the structure, and enrich character development.

CHEATS
While there are no subplots occurring in the script, there's certainly room to include one (or two). Not only will subplots help add depth to the narrative arc and theme, they'll also allow the audience to spend more time with some of the great secondary characters that have been created here too.
With the page count landing slightly under the expected length, consider adding in a subplot or two to help flesh the piece out, create more areas of conflict, and to show more variations on the central theme. There are certainly several interesting characters worth exploring further, and adding a subplot would help do this. (add suggestions on potential areas to explore in the story here too).
It's unusual to read a pilot script that contains no subplots, especially when the central conflict doesn't feel big enough to keep carrying the show. The writer may be missing the opportunity to explore secondary characters, create more obstacles, or to explore the theme from another angle by limiting the piece to just one plot thread here.

THERE ARE TOO MANY SUBPLOTS

This can often occur in scripts that feature a large ensemble cast and the writer is trying to ensure that everyone gets their moment to shine. Problems can occur when subplots are given too much setup and development, taking precious screen time away from the A-story, or when subplots are underdeveloped because of the lack of time, which can result in shallow characters who the audience don't get the time to connect with.

Advise the writer to revise the number of subplots they've used and question whether any could be amalgamated with others or cut altogether. Point out that too many subplots are potentially distracting the viewers from the main story. Of course, there could be the case that the A-story should play second fiddle to a stronger subplot, and you'll need to get the writer to ask themselves which thread or character are the audience more likely to want more of, but in general, ask the writer to consider sticking to three simple plot threads; the protagonist's plot, the supporting character's subplot, and the antagonist's subplot, in order to keep things simple but effective.

> **CHEATS**
>
> At present, the large cast and the multiple story threads risk cluttering the story as well as pulling the focus away from the central thread, suggesting that there are too many subplots crammed into this story. Keeping things simple by limiting the number of subplots and giving the central thread more screen time would help combat this.
>
> At times, it's easy to forget about the central plot because there are so many other story threads happening at the same time. Be aware that the protagonist risks being overshadowed by too many other subplots vying for attention. Consider limiting the number of subplots if this is a concern and dedicating more screen time to the protagonist.

SUBPLOTS AREN'T LINKED TO THE CENTRAL STORY

If subplots take the story off on a completely different tangent, don't link in any significant way to the A-story, and aren't mirroring the central theme, they'll make it feel like two or three separate films have been accidentally cut together to make one, which risks leaving the audience feeling confused and bewildered. The key word here is theme. Every subplot needs to reflect the overall meaning of the story by either supporting or contrasting with it.

Unconnected plot threads will also slow the pace of the A-story as well as compete with it, meaning viewers may be left wondering which thread they're really supposed to be following. Advise the writer that unless they better connect their subplots to the A-story, that they're potential cuts and recommend they either root them to the central theme or remove them.

> **CHEATS**
>
> While (secondary character's) subplot is (fun/interesting/unusual, etc.) as it doesn't quite tie in with the central thread, there's the risk that it could be cut altogether. Either make sure that this plot thread is showing a variation of the central theme or search for setups in this thread that you can pay off in the main thread to help knit them more tightly together.
>
> At this stage, (secondary character's) subplot sticks out, almost acting like a random short film that's playing alongside the central story because it isn't reflecting the central theme and nothing that occurs in this plot thread has any effect on the main storyline. Tying this subplot tighter to (the MC's) thread would ensure it doesn't get

SUBPLOTS DON'T MERGE DURING THE FINAL ACT

Every subplot should have its own beginning, middle, and end, and ideally it also needs to serve the central plot in some manner too, which usually comes into fruition when of all subplots merge during the third act (in a feature) or towards the end of a TV episode. Think of it as each subplot or thread being a setup that's later paid off in the main storyline. If this isn't happening, then it begs the question whether those subplots are adding anything worthy to the story or whether they're not being used to their full potential.

If you see this happening in a script, point it out to the reader, highlighting that they're possibly missing a great opportunity to tighten the entire script. Ask them to explore ways to add setups to subplots which can be later paid off during the end climax. This could be anything from separated characters being reunited, a skill learned in one thread becoming pivotal in another, or lessons being learned by the parties from each subplot that help convey the theme. If subplots and B-stories aren't adding anything to the main thread, they're probably space-filling scenes that should be cut.

> **CHEATS**
>
> Tighten the script even further by creating some setups in the subplots which are then later paid off in the main plot thread during the final act. This not only makes the subplots more effective and useful; it means that there's no need to cram so much into the A-story, allowing more time for character development.
>
> If subplots don't merge during the final act, questions may be raised about what purpose they serve, which risks them being cut from the script. Look for any potential setups in each subplot that could be paid off in the primary thread. This could be anything from a lesson being learned by a secondary character that later helps the MC win, a clue or important piece of info being discovered that leads (the MC) to (the climax location), or simply characters reuniting to beat (the antagonist). Knitting the subplots together more tightly will help produce a more satisfying story.

NARRATIVE DEVICES

Narrative (or plot) devices help to tell a story well. They're the additional elements that can elevate a basic story and they're anything that helps to drive the story forward, that elicits emotions in the audience, directs attention, or reveals information, etc. The most common narrative devices include flashbacks, foreshadowing, montages, dream sequences, cliff-hangers, a race against time, and red herrings, but they also include a Chekhov's gun (where every detail is essentially pivotal to the story in some manner), deus ex machina (when a seemingly unsolvable problem is suddenly resolved in an unexpected or coincidental manner), death traps (an antagonist's elaborate way to off the MC), and in medias res (breaking the linear narrative to start a story at a pivotal part, rather than at the beginning). There are of course lots more which are worth being aware of to help you identify them in a script.

More often than not, it's a lack of narrative devices in a script that's going to draw your attention, but when narrative devices are done badly, they're fairly obvious to spot too.

Consider making a comment if;

FLASHBACKS ARE USED UNNECESSARILY

Flashbacks flip-flop from being seen as welcome additions to a screenplay to being an easy cheat that indicates sloppy storytelling, and everyone seems to have their own opinions on them. If they're adding to the story by delivering info that we absolutely could only see in a flashback scene, then yes, they're enhancing the story. If the exposition that's being given could easily be delivered in a present scene, they don't raise the stakes in any way, or they're used too frequently, that's when it's worth highlighting there may be an issue to the writer.

Inserting a flashback can interrupt the narrative flow, especially when they're inserted at the wrong moment or have just been added to make the piece seem more interesting. A random flashback thrown into the middle of a sequence can feel slightly jarring, especially if the device is then never used again. Similarly, jumping back and forth between the present and the past can cause just as much interruption, so you'll need to make a judgment on whether a writer needs to establish more flashbacks or to cut back (or restructure) them instead.

There's also a judgement call to be made regarding delivering exposition. When we're throwing advice such as 'show, don't tell' at writers, it's easy to understand why they then use flashbacks to do just this. Consider the pace of the sequence, does the flashback feel out of place, how much time is the flashback taking up, what new info is being revealed, will the audience appreciate the visual reminder (if that's the purpose of the flashback), and are the stakes being raised?

Flashbacks should be treated no differently than scenes. They still need to be advancing the plot, delivering necessary information, revealing character, or at least be entertaining. If any flashbacks aren't doing this, make sure to inform the writer.

CHEATS

Flashbacks are useful for several reasons, but in general, if the info being expressed could easily be delivered during a present-tense scene, then there's every chance that the flashback isn't needed.

> **CHEATS CONT.**
>
> There's the argument that the flashbacks aren't needed in this script. While they're working well to (positive comment), they're not used consistently, making them feel like an all too easy plot device. Either establish flashbacks as a regular tool by adding more, or consider revealing the info they give during a present-tense scene instead.
>
> While the flashbacks work well to create visual breaks in the story, the flip-flopping from one time period to another is causing breaks in the dramatic momentum. Keep the intended emotion and reactions of the audience in mind and assess whether the timeline jumps are helping or hindering this.

MONTAGES DON'T ADVANCE THE PLOT

For a while, montages started to be considered as a little bit of a cheat (much in the same way that flashbacks were thought of by some), which were used to throw in a lot of information in a short amount of time, but when done well, montages can be hugely effective narrative devices, unfortunately, in amateur scripts, they can often be tedious to read, be used far too frequently, and don't add much to the story either.

Montages usually show the passage of time, speed through the story quickly, establish relationships between characters, or are used to compare and contrast two characters. In other words, a montage is either showing character development or plot development, but if it isn't doing either, then it's probably wasting space in a script, and it's not like montages don't already take up a lot of page space, right? (There are several different ways to format a montage, so only make a comment if the writer has used a really unorthodox or distracting way of doing it.)

Point out to the writer that montages have to be just as memorable as the rest of their script, otherwise they risk being skimmed over by the reader, which risks pivotal info being missed. The key is 'pivotal info' here. Filling up a montage with a series of uninteresting shots with no progression is slowing the pace, which precisely defeats the purpose of a montage in the first place. Every image, action, and line needs to have a purpose. The writer risks losing the interest of the viewers if they don't.

> **CHEATS**
>
> There are (a few/several/some, etc.) montages that don't feel particularly effective or memorable, meaning that they risk being skim read, overlooked, or missed entirely during the read. Adding a pivotal piece of information into every shot will ensure its need to be kept in the script.
>
> The series of shots montage is a potential cut as it feels more like a time-filling moment rather than a plot progressing one. Montages work best when they show a progression, so make sure the montage does this, or consider removing it altogether.
>
> At present, the series of shots occurring within the montage(s) aren't working hard enough to move the story forward, and this risks stagnating the pace, or worse, losing the audience's attention. Ensure to deliver new and pivotal information, create memorable visuals, and do enough to keep the read engaging during each montage if possible.

INFO IS REVEALED IN THE WRONG ORDER

This is another easy to spot error when reading as you'll have stopped the read in order to re-evaluate something after the writer has suddenly disclosed some pivotal info way too late in the script. Some common examples would be when a writer didn't mention a characters age, race, or need-to-know physical description when first introducing them, so it comes as a bit of a surprise when a few pages later you discover that the image you'd created in your mind is completely wrong after this new info is given.

The viewers need to know what they're looking at on the screen *before* they hear a character talking (or any other audio), even if it's only a black screen, so if a writer has started a scene with dialogue instead of scene description, they're revealing info in the wrong order too. Sometimes a character will abruptly start speaking during a scene without the writer even mentioning that they were there in the first place, and it's instances like these that cause the reader to stop, question logic, and that means that the immersion into the story has been broken too, which is something a writer needs to avoid.

Highlight to the writer that they risk causing confusion for the reader, which breaks immersion into the story, by not disclosing pivotal information in the correct order. Use specific examples from the script here to help the writer understand. As soon as something important appears on screen, it needs to be mentioned in the script, not ten-pages down the line.

> **CHEATS**
>
> Make sure to reveal information in the correct order to avoid causing confusion. Take (example from the script), for instance, which is something that the audience/reader really needs to be aware of much earlier.
>
> We need to know what we can see on screen before any audio is described in the script, so detail the visuals, even if that's only a black screen, before adding any sound.
>
> Remember to tell us what we can see on screen in the order that we see it. There's no point telling us (example from the script) (however many pages) after we've met this character. It's something we need to know as soon as they appear on the screen and on the page.

THE READER HASN'T UTILIZED THE 'RULE OF THREE'

We naturally look for patterns in life and three is the smallest unit needed to create a pattern. The 'Rule of Three' is used all the time in screenwriting. Structurally, it's the beginning, middle, and end. There are three acts, love triangles have three characters, franchises mostly come in trilogies, and if something happens twice in a story, you better believe the audience is expecting it to happen a third, and this makes it a great tool for writers. There's setup, anticipation, then payoff, which can be a punchline, a resolution, or plot twist.

You'll need to keep track of what you think might be a setup when first reading a script and look out for the payoffs as you go along. A trio of events can be more satisfying for the viewers, but perhaps there's a pivotal piece of exposition that was mentioned once or twice but needs a third mention to ensure that the viewers will be sure to pick up on it. Maybe a joke, pun, or catchphrase is being repeated one time too many, which ruins the effect. There's a thin line between repeating things for effect and overdoing it, which can result in treating the audience as fools

When the Rule of Three isn't being fulfilled, you'll notice it straight away, just because this structure has been somewhat culturally ingrained into most of us, but a writer who is too close to their own script or who have possibly cut away an intrinsic line or scene to shorten the page count, might not be able to see the break in pattern. Point out that adhering to the rule could lead to a more rewarding experience for the audience, help strengthen the structure, and tighten the plot at the same time too.

CHEATS

There are a couple of instances where applying the 'Rule of Three' would help to enhance the plot structure. Take (example from the script), for instance, which risks being (overkill/underkill). Audiences naturally expect three instances of (event/line/action, etc.), because it easily mimics the beginning, middle, and end structure that we're all familiar with, making a more satisfying experience, so consider (cutting back/adding another) instance here.

Three instances of (event/line/action from the script) creates a satisfying sequence, but (four or more) risks overkill, so consider adhering to the 'Rule of Three' in order to avoid running the (gag/event/line, etc.) dry.

CHARACTER

At its essence, just about every great story is character driven. A situation or event on its own isn't enough to make a story compelling. Instead, it's watching characters react and deal with a situation that grips us.

Again, start with some positives regarding the cast and protagonist. Name their strengths and weaknesses, how they fit within the genre, what will make the audience want to follow them on their journey, what did the writer do to make them relatable, unique, or interesting etc.? Begin with the protagonist. Point out their main personality traits and why they'll make this character exciting/engaging/relatable. The same applies to the antagonist. If there is one, what made them a worthy opponent? What traits can we empathize with? What's unique about them?

> **CHEATS**
>
> All of the characters are well crafted and are three-dimensional, each with their own flaws and strengths, all of which really help to flesh out the story.
>
> (the MC) may be (detail negative traits of this character) but the writer has done really well to establish empathy for this complex character early on by (example from the script).
>
> (the MC) is at the heart of this character piece, and the writer has done well to make them engaging, root-able, and flawed. With a good mix of tragedy, humor, and high-emotion happening throughout, this role contains plenty of actor bait that will hopefully attract major talent.
>
> (the MC) is the star of the show here. They're (list some positive attributes), all of which will make the audience warm to this character very quickly and ensure they'll want to keep following them on their journey.

CHARACTER INTRODUCTIONS

How a writer introduces their characters on the page can really affect the way a reader engages and visualizes them, but it's something that lots of writers neglect to do well. Introducing a character is an opportunity to set the tone, reveal a character's emotional need, and it's where the audience are hooked into following them.

Consider making a comment if;

PHYSICAL APPEARANCES ARE TOO DETAILED

Unless a character's sweater and jeans play a significant part in the plot, a writer doesn't need to include them in their screenplay. The same applies to hairstyles, tattoos, jewelry, or any physical descriptions that aren't really adding anything to the story. Telling us that a character is blonde with hazel brown eyes, for example, isn't revealing personality, it's limiting the casting opportunities, it's taking up unnecessary space on the page, slowing the read, and it's not moving the story forward.

Encourage writers to describe a character's overall style. This can help reveal a character's attitude, identity, and personality without the writer doing the costume department's job for them in the process. Mentioning a character's occupation could be enough to evoke what they'll be wearing, and if they do need to include specifics, make sure they're pivotal to the plot and are setups to later payoffs.

CHEATS

Unless it's essential to the plot that (character) is wearing (description from the script), it doesn't need to be included in the script. Either make a point of using clothing to reveal something essential about a character or add an essence statement instead, which tells the reader and actor more about who this person is as opposed to what they look like.

Avoid wasting time over-detailing each character's physical appearance. Not only does this limit the casting choices, physical attributes don't work particularly well to reveal much about who a character is, their attitudes, ethos, or personalities, etc.

Minimizing the amount of unnecessary info given will help increase the pace. Is it really pivotal to the plot that (character) wears (description from the script), for example, or that (another instance from the script)? Unless those details are essential to the story, these descriptions are cluttering up the page and are potential cuts.

VITAL INFORMATION IS MISSING

Age is going to be the obvious vital piece of info that's missing when a character is introduced. There's conflicting advice out there for writers, who may have read that adding an age limits the casting possibilities of a role, but if there's nothing else in the description to indicate a character's age, ultimately, it's misleading the reader.

"JANE lounges on the couch, scrolling through her phone" for instance, could easily be a teenage girl, a middle-aged socialite, a retired lady of leisure, or anything in between. If the reader has painted the image of a character in their mind and that abruptly gets changed four or five pages later, everything that the reader has surmised about that character then needs to be revised, which is forcing the reader to do more work than they need to, and that's something any writer should avoid. Advise that the character they're describing could be interpreted in wildly different ways because of missing information, risking confusion, and to do more to paint a more accurate picture if possible.

CHEATS

It's well worth painting a strong visual picture of each of your core cast members as soon as we meet them on the page. Don't risk misleading the reader by leaving it too late to reveal important information, such as (example from the script), which feels like something we really need to know the moment we see this character, not (however many) pages later.

It's important to tell us what we can see on screen and in the order that we see it. There's the risk of causing disruption if it's left too late to deliver pivotal information, such as when we discover that (character) is (whatever was revealed too late and how many pages) after we first meet them, which is probably something we needed to know as soon as they're shown on screen.

Adding an age to all of the core cast can go a long way to build an accurate visual picture of them in the reader's mind. Don't feel that this is limiting casting options for the characters. It's all about making sure that the reader isn't being misled and avoiding any possible confusion when a character is assumed to be one age by the reader but it later becomes apparent that they were incorrect. (use an example from the script to highlight this point if possible).

ACTION ISN'T REVEALING CHARACTER

What a character is doing when we first meet them also needs to reveal who they are. The way they interact with other characters, make decisions, and the actions they take creates a starting point from which they grow. If a writer introduces a character doing a mundane task, classic examples are making breakfast, or the series of shots as they get ready for work sequence, they better be telling us why we should want to follow them at the same time too.

A writer needs to consider what the actions their characters are doing when we first meet them are telling us. What are we learning from watching "MARK (mid-30s), dressing gown, slippers, pours coffee and chews toast while KAREN (30) reads the morning news on her iPad."? Is it evoking personality, displaying their flaws, or revealing anything about their relationship?

CHEATS

When (character) is introduced, they're (action taking place in the script), but what is this telling us about this character, if anything? Don't forget to use actions as much as dialogue to establish who your characters are, especially when we first see them on screen.

We've all seen (cliched introduction from the script) countless times before, and while yes, this grounds the character(s) in a familiar setting, there's also scope to make the moment we meet characters on screen much more original, visual, and memorable.

Carefully consider what the actions a character takes reveals about them, especially during the scenes when they're first introduced. Look for ways to show personality, attitude, ethos, culture, background, etc., through action, rather than relying on the dialogue. It's worth considering how to *show* us who (character) is, instead of telling us.

GENDER ISN'T IMMEDIATELY CLEAR

Giving unisex names to characters isn't a problem unless it takes an entire page, or longer, for the reader to figure out that the character they've already envisaged in their head is a completely different gender. Readers may read multiple screenplays in a day, so anything that isn't instantly recognizable may go amiss. If you, as the reader, mistook a character's gender because of an androgynous name, then there's a high chance other readers will do too. If it causes confusion, advise the writer change the name or do more to visually evoke the character on the page.

> **CHEATS**
>
> Make sure to give all the necessary information straight away when introducing characters. It's not abundantly obvious that (character) is (gender) when we first meet them, so avoid any possible confusion by detailing this as quickly as possible.
>
> It wasn't until (number of pages) after (character) was introduced that it became clear that they were (gender), which leaves plenty of time for a reader to have already created an image of this character in their mind. Don't risk the reader having to correct their initial assumptions by delivering this necessary information as soon as they're introduced on the page.

CHARACTER NAMES ARE CONFUSING

There's the risk that characters will be easily confused with one another if they have similar sounding names. Rob, Rod, and Robin. Joan, Jane, and Janet. Sandy, Mandy, and Andy, etc. Even names that look different on the page but sound similar when spoken should be avoided, such as Craig and Greg.

While there's the temptation to have unique and memorable character names, if they are too unusual, there's going to be every chance that they'll be skim read or mispronounced. Of course, there are certain genres where unusual names are expected, such as fantasy and sci-fi, in which case, advise that shorter is better.

Long names take longer to type, read, pronounce, as well as taking up more space on the page, so if a writer has gone into overkill with double-barreled or titled names, advise them it's to their advantage to shorten them so that they're both easier to read and remember. This doesn't mean using creative spellings, such as Mykel, Jazz-Myn, or Alys, which again, some readers may struggle to digest easily.

It can also be difficult to keep track of who is saying what during scenes with numbered characters who appear in more than one scene in the script.

SECURITY GUARD #1, SECURITY GUARD #2, SECURITY GUARD #3 etc. end up blurring into one another when a reader is trying to read a script as quickly as possible, so advise the writer adds in a descriptive element that will help each character stand out from one another, such as AGEING GUARD, COCKY GUARD, or NERVOUS GUARD, etc.

> **CHEATS**
>
> Try to avoid having characters with similar-sounding names. (examples from the script) all (look/sound) far too alike, meaning it's easy to mix these characters up when reading. Avoid this by giving them much more varied names.
>
> With so many numbered characters, it's easy to lose track of who is doing what throughout the story. Adding a description to help the reader recognize individual characters on the page, such as (suggestions from the reader) would help to avoid this.
>
> The imaginative names of the cast are certainly creative and unique, but be aware, they're also a bit too far on the unfamiliar side, which makes them easy to mispronounce and a mouthful to say, both of which make them highly-skimmable words on the page, which can lead to pivotal details being missed by the reader.

MAJOR CHARACTERS HAVEN'T BEEN NAMED

If there's a character who plays a pivotal role in the story and has a significant amount of screen time but is called by an uninspiring, impersonal, or insignificant name, such as their job role, physical description, or relation to another character, then it lessens that character's function in the story. I've noticed a trend where this seems to apply more to female characters than with male ones, where a character is simply called HUGH'S MOTHER, MRS. HARRIS (if they're the MC's wife), or GIRLFRIEND, making these characters feel more like useful props in the story rather than interesting characters in their own right. Plus, names like this are unlikely to attract talent to the play those roles.

> **CHEATS**
>
> (character) certainly plays a significant part in this story, which makes not giving them a name an unusual choice. Don't diminish this part by generalizing their name and making the character feel more like a prop, which doesn't do much to make the role appealing to talent either.

CHARACTERS ARE NUMBERED INSTEAD OF NAMED

It's absolutely fine to do this if there's one or two minor characters who only appear briefly, but if a script is riddled with numbered characters, such as, SECURITY GUARD #1, CONSTRUCTION WORKER #2, or FLIGHT ATTENDANT #3, not only is the writer using long-winded character names in their script that take up way too much space on the page, they're also risking one character being mistaken for another. More important than that, the reader won't be terribly emotionally engaged with these characters. Numbered characters can easily blend into one another and act more like disposable props in the story as opposed to real characters.

Advise the writer that they either need to cut back or amalgamate the number of extras they have in their script, which will help to cut the budget, and to personalize characters who feature in more than one or two scenes, thus bringing them to life for the reader.

> **CHEATS**
>
> It's hard to (connect with/picture/recognize, etc.) a numbered character on the page, so consider personalizing characters who are named in this manner by adding a description that helps them feel more individual, such as (suggestions from the reader).
>
> There's an excessive amount of numbered characters, which not only makes it hard to keep track of who is doing what, it's hard to connect with these nameless characters too. Consider cutting back on the amount of characters by reusing some them instead of introducing new ones, by amalgamating several characters into one person, or by removing any character that isn't particularly pivotal.

GOALS

The protagonist should always have a clearly defined goal established for them during Act I and ideally, one that the audience is going to be interested in. Technically, a protagonist can have two goals; the thing that they *want*, and the thing that they *need*, and in a perfect world, they both should conflict with one another. The 'want' is the story's basic plot. It's to get the girl, to exact revenge, to survive etc., but the 'need' is a deeper subconscious desire that the character may or may not realize they have, and is often referred to as the underlying motivation behind their want.

While the 'want' is usually a physical desire that the MC believes will be the answer to all of their problems, the 'need' is often a realization of some sort, such as the lesson they learned along the way. It's a common structural formula for the protagonist to finally gain what they wanted all along only to discover that it wasn't the real success they were looking for, and the realization that they had the one thing they *really* wanted (aka the 'need') all along, but just didn't realize it.

Consider making a comment if;

THE MC HAS NO CLEAR GOAL

This is a common issue in scripts if the character is passive or the story is about characters experiencing an everyday event or 'slice of life' story, but not having a clear goal can cause a multitude of issues further down the line. If we don't know what the protagonist wants, how will we know whether they've achieved it, and how can we root for them to succeed if we don't know what they're trying to do?

The MC's goal or problem needs to be stated as quickly as possible, not left until the second act, or worse, never stated at all, but if a writer's forgotten about including one in their script, remind them that the audience has to have a firm reason to want to follow their character. Sure, you can have a likeable character that the audience will easily warm to, but if they have nothing to aim for, nothing to fight against, or no purpose, then they're going be become pretty boring, pretty fast. If they're not actively driving the plot forward; then the plot is happening around them, which means there's no conflict – the central foundation of every story.

> **CHEATS**
>
> At this stage, it's hard to ascertain what (the MC's) primary goal is, especially during the all-important first act, where the audience needs to know who they're following, what big problem they face, what's standing in their way, and why they should care. If we don't know what (MC) is trying to achieve, how will the viewers know if the goal has been reached or not?
>
> Understandably, this is a 'slice of life' story, where there's no outward goal set for (the MC), and while this can work well, there's also the risk that if the audience doesn't have a reason to care about this character, will they be invested enough to keep following them? Constructing a goal, even a minor one, will help the viewers not only root more for (the MC), but to connect to them too.
>
> A character doesn't always need to have a clear goal at the beginning of a story, but it's a huge help in getting the audience to root for them. If there's no goal, it makes it harder to understand what's motivating a character, what's driving them forward, what their end game is, etc. Establishing a clear goal will also help to construct more effective obstacles to throw in the way, so it's definitely something to consider including here.

THE MC'S GOAL ISN'T INTERESTING ENOUGH

When a goal is boring, it's often due to the fact that there are no major stakes involved. The audience has got to care whether the protagonist overcomes their problem, but if there are no compelling stakes involved, what's going to make the task interesting? Knowing what the MC is willing to give up or risks losing should they fail can help make them more relatable as it allows the audience to understand what's motivating them. A boring goal can be made more interesting by having high stakes at risk with creative obstacles standing in the way, but a boring goal with little preventing it from being achieved or with nothing to lose if it's not reached won't satisfy audiences.

Recommend that the writer either creates a more interesting or relatable goal for the protagonist, or try to spice up a lackluster one by making that goal extremely difficult to achieve, having it be very important to the MC, and including huge consequences should they fail.

> **CHEATS**
>
> While the writer has successfully established a clear goal for (the MC), is it compelling enough to grab the audience's undivided attention and make them want to keep watching? Heightening the stakes is one way to hook the viewers further, so consider either making the goal more riveting or creating bigger consequences for (the MC) should they fail to achieve it.
>
> Consider heightening the initial goal that (MC) has to achieve, especially during the first act, just to ensure that the audience is gripped enough by it to continue watching. As it stands, is (current goal) going to be (big/interesting/compelling, etc.) enough to hook them? Increasing the stakes, making the goal extremely important to (the MC), or turning the goal into something that the viewers can relate to on an emotional level would all allow the audience to really get behind (the MC) and want to see them succeed.

THE MC'S MOTIVATIONS ARE UNCLEAR

If a character's motivations are unclear, the audience may struggle to understand why they're taking the actions that they do. Understanding what the driving force is behind every action not only makes it easier to emotionally connect with a character, it makes them more believable too. If you find that a character is making implausible decisions, it could be due to some pivotal background information that's missing. This doesn't mean inserting a clumsy flashback or using exposition-heavy voice over by any means. It could be something as short and simple as showing a gambling addict have a small win in order to visually explain why they're spending money they don't have, a jealous glance towards a colleague who's just got a promotion to help explain a murder motive, or lacking confidence in a role they're destined to fulfill.

If a character is determined to leave home, but there is no clear reason for them wanting to do so, it makes it hard for the audience to really get behind them and to root for their success. If we see an abusive parent, a manipulative step-sibling, or a horrendous lack of privacy etc., then the reasons for wanting to leave become much easier (and relatable) to understand. Remind a writer that if the MC's motivations behind their goal aren't clear, then they're missing the opportunity to have the audience emotionally engage with their protagonist, and they could be risk creating confusion or worse, push the limits of believability too far for the viewers.

CHEATS
It's worth doing more to reveal the motivations behind (characters) actions, as at certain times, such as (example from the script), this feels like an (illogical/uncharacteristic/improbable, etc.) action to take. Without understanding what's prompted (character) to do this, will the audience swallow it?
Be careful not to bend the realms of believability by having characters make too many implausible decisions. Providing some (backstory/insight/revelations, etc.) on what's motivating these characters to take the actions they do would really help add credibility and ensure that the audience keeps following.
Don't forget to tell us what's motivating your protagonist throughout their journey. Understanding what's prompting them to make the decisions they do will not only increase the stakes, it'll also help to build empathy from the audience, making them want to root for (the MC) even more.

FLAWS, WEAKNESSES, AND LIMITATIONS

Giving character's one major flaw (alongside several smaller ones) helps to transform them into more relatable, three-dimensional, and realistic people, but it's not uncommon for rookie writers to create near-perfect heroes who easily overcome every obstacle, make all the right decisions, and are just too-good-to-be-true, creating a pretty boring and unrealistic story.

Character flaws don't just have to be negative personality traits, quirks, biases, or false beliefs. They can also be intertwined or replaced by a weakness or limitation instead. Superman's weakness is Kryptonite, the Wicked Witch of the West was vulnerable to water, and Professor X is limited by being in a wheelchair, for example.

As with stakes, it's a good idea for the writer to show the audience what negative effects a flaw has on the MC's life. If a character's weakness is their unbridled passion for destruction derby racing, then the writer probably should show us how this enthusiasm has resulted in ruined relationships, reckless endangerment, or loss of income etc. in order to display exactly why it's a flaw in the first place, but if you're reading a script where there are no discernible scenes expressing a character flaw that would help the audience empathize, relate to, or understand the decisions that character is making, then you need to highlight that more character development is needed.

Consider making a comment if;

THE MC IS TOO PERFECT

A writer may be worried that the audience won't like someone who is flawed or has weaknesses, but this couldn't be further from the truth. If a character is too perfect, they're probably overcoming challenges relatively easily, meaning that tension, suspense, and drama will be lacking, resulting in a boring and predictable story. It's also going to be a lot harder for the audience to relate to a character like this. Part of the reason characters have flaws in the first place is so that the audience can see something of themselves in them, to empathize with them, and to have a good reason to root for them, but if an MC is too perfect, there's more chance of the audience disliking them than loving them.

A prefect character may also have a rather weak arc because they won't have really changed by the end of their journey. You can't improve on perfection, after all, and a protagonist without a powerful character arc may leave a movie feeling rather unsatisfying. Encourage the writer to consider creating a central flaw or weakness for their MC not only to turn them into a more three-dimensional character, but to also add in new layers of conflict and make them more relatable. The more the flaw ties in with the central conflict of the plot, the better, such as a sheriff with a fear of water being tasked with hunting down a killer shark, a ruthless lawyer who must get through the day unable to tell a lie, or a man-child reluctant to face responsibility who accidentally knocks up a one-night stand.

> **CHEATS**
>
> At present, (the MC) is easily overcoming obstacles, solving problems, and rarely feels challenged in any manner, and while this makes them extremely competent, it also risks them being extremely boring at the same time too. Giving them a weakness, flaw, or limitation will help add more conflict as well as make (the MC) much more interesting to watch.

> **CHEATS CONT.**
>
> By making (the MC) too perfect to begin with, the opportunity to create some rewarding character development has been missed. Consider giving them at least one major character flaw, which can then be used to indicate character growth along the way. This will help make them more relatable, realistic, and engaging for the audience.
>
> Audiences don't want to see everything handed to the hero on a plate. They want to see them struggle, flounder, and fail along the way. By making (the MC) far too (competent/confident/capable, etc.) the opportunity to create more conflict, challenges, and character growth has been missed.

THE MAJOR FLAW ISN'T TIED TO THE CENTRAL PLOT

Flawed characters are great. They're more relatable, more three-dimensional, and more believable, but when a character has a negative trait that doesn't directly influence the story, there's going to be the argument about why it's really needed. Sometimes it can feel like a random flaw has just been thrown in to be used only once, then forgotten about. Being clumsy is a frequent example of a flaw that's established. It's usually to put the character into a situation where they need to be saved, but is then never used again, making it a convenient one-off.

Take *Flubber* (1997), which was a remake of *The Absent-Minded Professor* (1961), except we only see Prof Brainard's forgetfulness during the first fifteen-minutes of *Flubber*, and it's magically never an issue ever again. Similarly, in *Captain Marvel* (2019) where we're told early on that Carol is too emotional and subsequently can't control her powers because of it, yet we're never shown an example of this actually happening during the rest of the movie, bar an arguably controlled outburst wrecking a computer. Both examples highlight an initial character flaw that was either used once and forgotten about or was an overly convenient plot device.

Inserting onetime flaws can come across as being disingenuous, so either the writer needs to continue to use that flaw to impede the primary problem, or they need to change it to one that will. Suggesting that the writer work backwards by examining what the MC's goal is and figuring out what particular flaw might cause the most problems when trying to achieve it might be an idea here. Often a great flaw is the direct opposite of a character's strength.

> **CHEATS**
>
> There's scope to knit the plot even tighter together by utilizing (the MC) central flaw more than just that one single time to create further conflict.
>
> Consider using (the MC) major flaw more frequently throughout the script and tying it closer to the central plot of the story. This will prevent the (character flaw) from feeling like an overly convenient plot device that's been thrown in just for the one single scene.
>
> Having (the MC) be (flawed) is a great way to make this character feel realistic and believable, but as this flaw only really causes problems during one scene, has the opportunity to fully utilize this flaw been missed? Consider how this flaw could cause further problems for (the MC) during other pivotal scenes, which will help add even more conflict and more rewarding setups and payoffs for the viewers.

THE MC'S WEAKNESS DOESN'T BECOME A STRENGTH

A great way to show character growth is by transforming the flaw or weakness that held the MC back during the first act into a strength that helps them win the final battle in the third act. Exploiting a flaw and using it to foreshadow what the protagonist has to later defeat, overcome, or face (both internally and externally), can really help tighten a story and make it a much more fulfilling experience. When a character is able to overcome their central flaw, it shows us they've changed, which in turn completes their character arc.

In order to get the writer to explore this idea, get them to think about what positive skills their flaw could create. Say you have a character whose flaw/weakness is being an addict. Their addiction has resulted in them losing their job, wrecked their relationships, and put them in serious debt, etc. But that addictive personality also gives them relentless determination, they're not afraid to take big chances, and it maybe even allows them to think outside of the box when trying to get what they want. All of which could be used when they're trying to achieve whatever goal has been established during the first act. While a flaw initially needs to get in the way of a character achieving their goal, if there's an opportunity to flip it 180° and make it a source of power, the writer should take it.

CHEATS

It's worth exploring ways to further use (the MC) central flaw during the third act, which is a great way to show more character development, especially if (the MC) learns to turn their flaw into a strength that helps to overcome the (antagonistic character or force).

(protagonists) weakness is used well to create some nice conflict throughout the plot, but they never truly overcome this flaw, begging the question, would it help to tighten the plot further if that weakness got turned into a strength by the end of the story?

Does (the MC) need to somehow overcome their (weakness/flaw/limitation) in order to help show more character development? What lessons learned along the way could help them to adapt the one thing that's been holding them back all this time into the one thing that helps them overcome their greatest obstacle?

STAKES

One of the most common mistakes that writer's make is to forget about creating stakes for their characters, but in an otherwise enjoyable script, it can easily go unnoticed by an inexperienced reader. Creating stakes gives the audience a reason to want to see the protagonist succeed, and if they're not compelling enough, there's the risk that the audience won't care whether the MC is successful or not, and that risks them losing interest.

Consider making a comment if;

THERE ARE NO CLEAR STAKES

Understanding what's at risk should the MC fail is pivotal in helping the viewers to root for that character. If there are no disastrous consequences if the protagonist doesn't win, then it makes no difference whether they succeed or not, meaning that there's no real purpose to their actions. Stakes need to be stated as early as possible within the first act, and equally, at some stage, we also need to know what's at stake for the antagonist, as well as every secondary character in there too, so this isn't just an issue for the MC.

If the stakes aren't clear, you need to point out to the writer that they're missing a great opportunity to heighten the conflict and to emotionally engage with the audience, who will otherwise feel less sympathetic for the characters they're supposed to be rooting for. Introducing the stakes also introduces conflict, and conflict is the cornerstone of every great story.

Whatever the stakes are, they need to be extremely important to the character. There's no point having a character put their job on the line if they're from a wealthy family and don't need the money, or have a protagonist risk losing their spouse if they're cheating on them anyway, etc. They've got to really care about whatever it is they have to lose, otherwise why should the audience care either? The more personal the stake is, the more the viewers will engage and relate, so connecting the MC's stakes to their 'inner need' as much as their 'external goal' can be very powerful.

CHEATS
Without knowing what (the MC) stands to lose should they fail; will the audience have a big enough reason to keep following this character?
Has the opportunity to encourage the audience to root for (the MC) been missed by not establishing exactly what they risk losing should they fail?
If we don't know what the protagonist stands to lose, should they fail their quest, will the audience care enough to want to follow this character on their journey?
Consider inserting some clear stakes for (the MC) during the first act to add more importance to their goal. This will allow the viewers to better understand what's motivating every action they take, plus it'll also generate some much-needed empathy for them too.

THE STAKES AREN'T BIG ENOUGH

Yes, it's possible to have a low-stake story. Not every protagonist needs to have the possibility of their life being ruined, their loved one killed, or be in danger of imminent death for the story to be compelling, but low-stake stories still need to keep the audience interested. This can be achieved by using a combination of compelling characters who really care about achieving their goal and a series of inventive problems for them to overcome. That said, it's fairly uncommon to read screenplays like this, especially amateur ones, and if the stakes aren't big enough, does it really matter if the MC achieves their goal or not, and will the viewers even care?

Remind the writer; the higher the stakes, the easier it is for the viewers to relate and identify with a character, so they need to understand just how awful life will be for the protagonist should they fail in their quest and as usual, this needs to be established as quickly as possible. If it's a character's day job to solve a problem, such as an ethical hacker trying to prevent a cyber heist, or some other faceless problem, it can be hard to make the stakes feel compelling, so advise the writer to add in a personal stake for the MC too. If the problem is going to have a personal or emotional impact on their lives in some manner, such as the cyber-criminals also wiping out the hackers poorly mother's bank account, or the cyber-criminal just happens to be the hackers jaded protégé, thus making him feel personally responsible, then the MC has a bigger emotional connection to the problem, which can work well to raise the stakes to a higher level in the process.

CHEATS

At present, (the MC) doesn't stand to lose a great deal should they fail. They can easily (go back to their old life with little consequence), and this lessens the tension, immediacy, and the importance of (the quest). Heighten the stakes to make the audience care more about whether (the MC) succeeds or not here.

If the protagonist really cares about their quest, so will the audience, but at this stage, the protagonist only stands to lose (small stake). Adding a big personal stake would help heighten the tension, drive the motivation, and generate more empathy for (the MC) here.

> **CHEATS CONT.**
>
> If the stakes aren't high enough, the audience may find it hard to care if the hero succeeds or not. Heightening the stakes would avoid this. What's the worst thing that could happen to the protagonist if they fail, both professionally, emotionally, and personally?
>
> Don't forget to tell the audience just how awful (the MC) life is going to be if they don't achieve (their goal). If we don't know what drastic consequences lie in wait should they fail, will the audience care enough to invest in this character?

THE STAKES DON'T INCREASE THROUGHOUT

The initial stake will sometimes only keep the viewers excited for so long, so adding to the tension as the story advances not only stops the audience from getting bored, it makes them want to see the MC win all the more. Writers at any stage of their career will often come up against the post-midpoint lull, where the story almost seems to run out of steam, but this is exactly where things should be ramping up a gear. If you sense this in a script, increasing the stakes could be a great way to solve the problem.

There are several ways to increase the stakes, from amplifying the physical dangers, losing an advantage that the MC had, adding a ticking time-bomb element, or forcing a character to make an impossible decision, etc., but it's not your job to come up with the solution for the writer. Make the point that the lack of intensifying stakes is stopping the dramatic momentum that's been gained up until that point and it's probably also leaving the protagonist without an 'all is lost' moment too, which can be pivotal in both getting the audience to really care about the character as well as showing an important moment of growth for the MC. Advise they keep creating bigger and more challenging obstacles as much as possible.

> **CHEATS**
>
> Although there's a good attempt to remind the viewers what the protagonist stands to lose throughout the story, don't forget to also keep increasing the stakes along the way too. If things stay the same for too long, there's the risk that the audience will become less interested.

Character | 115

> **CHEATS CONT.**
>
> There's a noticeable lull in the action and drama at (specific point). Increasing the stakes would be one way to avoid losing the viewers' attention there.
>
> If the stakes don't increase as the story moves forward, there's the risk that the original stake loses its impact and interest for the audience. Upping the stakes throughout to continually engage with the viewers, to keep them on their toes, and to leave them wanting more, is advised.

ROOT-ABILITY

We're used to seeing protagonists being likeable characters with flaws that make them relatable and human, but as audiences have become more sophisticated, watching unlikable character's (or anti-heroes) with one or two positive attributes that help us root for them is also becoming popular. Overly flawed characters or redemption stories, where a character transforms from very unlikeable to likable by the end, both run the risk of not getting the reader on side during those early scenes where the writer is trying to establish the MC as an awful person, so it's important that writers also create strong reasons as to why we'd want to follow even the most loathsome of characters.

In essence, if the audience doesn't care about the character they're supposed to be following, they won't be emotionally invested, and they'll be left feeling unsatisfied.

Consider making a comment if;

THE MC IS TOO UNLIKABLE

It's a myth that protagonists need to be likable, but they do need to be compelling. Sometimes a writer unwittingly doesn't realize that the characters they've created can come across as unlikable by the audience. Privileged characters, for example, who've already had everything handed to them on a plate, or children who haven't really done anything to earn their status, can be difficult to relate to without us first seeing a moment of humanity, kindness, or a glimpse of vulnerability, etc. If a character isn't actively doing anything to win us over, and the writer is relying on the characters' good looks, wealth, or status to hook us, they might not get the results they expect.

If the protagonist of the script you're reading is hard to engage with, you need to let the writer know exactly why that is. If you're not connecting to them, there's a high chance others won't either. Encourage the writer to introduce a reason as to why we should want to follow their MC. There are many ways to do this, from giving the character a 'save the cat moment', making them funny, revealing a past trauma, or making the character feel regret, guilt, or fear, etc. Ultimately, if we don't like a character, there better be a compelling reason for us to want to keep watching them. Otherwise, they need to be made more relatable, induce our empathy, or our interest in some manner.

CHEATS

More consideration of how the audience will react to (the MC) should be kept in mind. Are they more likely to love or loathe them when they (example of the MC taking dubious action in the script)? While a story doesn't necessarily need to have a likable protagonist, there at least needs to be a good reason as to why the audience will want to follow them. Has it been left too late in the story for the audience to feel this way about (the MC)?

While (the MC) does eventually find redemption at the end, there's a high risk that the viewers may not have stuck around that long to see it. Consider giving this unlikable character a 'save the cat' moment or an instance showing some vulnerability, regret, or anything that's going to allow the audience to begin caring about (the MC) during the first act that will hook them enough into staying with this character for the rest of the journey.

At this stage, with no real (redeeming qualities/relatable flaws/challenging obstacles to overcome, etc.) the audience may find it difficult to root for (the MC), and this could be a major stumbling block when trying to pitch this project.

CHARACTERS ARE ONE-DIMENSIONAL

Stereotypes are immediately recognizable character types that can be useful when a writer needs to establish an individual in a very short period of time, so you'll often see them feature more in short films, comedies, or as minor character roles, but using them comes at a risk. Stereotypical characters are simplified personalities that are one-dimensional, lack any real depth, can come across as being offensive, and more importantly, they're not original. If a writer is relying too heavily on filling their cast with familiar stereotypes, they're also taking shortcuts when it comes to character design.

Advise writers to break stereotypes instead of including them. This can actually work really well to help create unique and memorable characters at the same time. Reversing expectations, adding diversity, or using archetypes instead of stereotypes can at least help to add more layers to a character and stop them from being just black or white.

CHEATS

At present, there's the risk that some characters are coming across as being slightly one-dimensional, meaning that they feel more like plot devices than relatable characters with depth. One-dimensional characters don't learn anything, don't change, and have no character arc, which can leave them feeling flat and predictable. Don't forget that secondary characters need to feel just as developed as the protagonist so that the audience will emotionally engage with them. Consider devoting more development time to these characters.

Consider fleshing (stereotypical characters) out a little more to avoid them being viewed as (flat/clichéd/unrealistic, etc.). Stereotypical characters can be useful, but in this instance, having cartoonish characters doesn't quite fit with the rest of the story.

A couple of the characters, such as (examples from the script) are verging on being stereotypical, which might work if this was a comedy, but it doesn't quite fit in a (genre of the script). Consider dialing back the clichéd (stereotype being used) and adding a little more depth to these characters to help make them more original and believable.

THE CAST LACKS DIVERSITY

Writer's shouldn't be adding in more diversity just for the sake of it; it still needs to work within the story world they've created. This can be particularly difficult with period pieces that want to stay true to history, but diversity isn't an issue that's going to go away, so advise writers use it to their advantage instead of viewing it as a restriction. Not only does Hollywood claim to be calling out for more diverse casts, diversity is also a great way to add more layers of conflict, culture, and realism to a story, so it's something a writer needs to consider if they want their script to be more appealing.

Writers don't need to be detailing what race each of their characters are or going overboard in describing them physically unless it's essential to the plot. Giving a character an ethnic name can go a long way to painting just as an effective picture while using fewer words on the page, but increasing diversity doesn't just mean including more gender or race variations in the cast, it also means including different cultures, attitudes, sexualities, or physical and mental disabilities. Audiences are looking for representation when they watch something. They want to relate, to empathize, to see themselves on screen, and to be inspired. A writer could box themselves into a corner if they're not willing to be diverse.

CHEATS

Would adding more diversity into the cast help create more mini-conflicts to help flesh things out even further? Consider how coming from another culture, having a challenging disability/limitation, be struggling with gender or sexuality, etc., might bring new conflicts, problems, or tests for these characters to face.

Would the piece benefit by reflecting a more accurate representation of contemporary life? At present, the cast is fairly typical, but this risks them being rather bland too. It's not about adding diversity just for the sake of it here, but consider what new challenges and conflicts could be created by including multi-layered characters who are also battling all too familiar prejudices that the audience can relate to.

IT'S UNCLEAR WHOSE STORY IT IS

Even if the script contains an ensemble cast or has dual protagonists, in most cases, there should be one character who can be clearly identified as the primary MC, but sometimes if there's a secondary character getting more screen time than the suspected protagonist or scenes focus on multiple POV's it can be hard to ascertain just who's story is being told.

You may need to ask a writer to make a firm decision about who they want their story to be about if it's not clear from the script. A writer may accidentally create more interesting personal stakes, a more rewarding character arc, or give more screen time to a secondary character, when ideally, it's the MC who should get all the glory. This begs the question of whether they've picked the wrong protagonist to begin with. Point out the pros and cons between choosing whichever potential protagonists there are, who has the more engaging journey, who will the audience want to root for more, who is the more active character etc. in order to help the writer gauge who they should focus on.

CHEATS

At present, it's not entirely clear who the protagonist is in this story, and that risks creating confusion for the viewers. (give reasons why the protagonist could be any of two or more characters). Consider who has the more interesting plot thread, who will the audience want to follow more, and who has the most to lose should the quest fail. Whichever character becomes the protagonist should ideally have more screen time than any other character.

There are mixed messages coming through about exactly who the audience should be following. The story starts off with (first character), indicating that they're the hero of the piece, but the focus then shifts towards (second character), and (first character) almost becomes forgotten about. It's worth figuring out who the protagonist of the piece is and making sure that they have the majority of screen time to avoid creating any confusion.

(first character) is the clear protagonist here as they have the most screen time but as (second character) has (more to lose/the more emotionally charged story thread/is a character the audience will root for more, etc.), does the story possibly focus on the wrong character?

CHARACTERS AREN'T EMOTIONALLY ENGAGING

At the end of the day, if the audience doesn't connect to the characters they're watching on an emotional level, the writer hasn't done their job terribly well. We don't always have to like a character, but we do need to empathize with them and we need to be interested in them enough to want to follow them on their journey. This means the viewers need to be able to identify with the characters in some manner, but often you'll read a script and be left thinking "I didn't really care whether the MC succeeded or not" or "There were no characters I could relate to". If this is happening in a script, it makes it very hard to keep turning the pages, and that's probably the worst thing a script can be.

Paying particular attention to the protagonist and the antagonist, you'll need to examine exactly why you weren't able to connect with the characters. You don't always have to immediately feel something when a character is first introduced, but that moment is certainly an area to look at. Does more empathy need to be generated for the character? Do we need to see them in an underdog position, be mistreated, or treated unjustly, etc.? Do they lack a weakness, limitation, or a flaw that would make them feel more realistic? Does the character lack any admirable traits, such as courage, honesty, or a sense of humor, which could help us warm to them more? Or does the character need to have more of an air of mystery about them? Do they act predictably, have no secrets we'll want to uncover, or talk on-the-nose, leaving nothing withheld?

There are lots of different ways to create emotionally engaging characters, but it's not your job to figure out which ones the writer should use. You can, however, suggest a selection that helps point the writer in the right direction. The important note to make is that every successful screenplay was able to emotionally connect with the reader, and if that's presently missing, it's a key element to fix.

CHEATS

There are numerous unlikable characters in this piece, and while that can definitely work in certain genres, such as a slasher movie, here, it's hard to really root for anyone. If the audience doesn't care about the characters on screen, there's the risk they'll stop watching. Consider giving the viewers a reason to want to see these characters succeed by building empathy for them in some manner.

> **CHEATS CONT.**
>
> At present, it may be difficult for the audience to emotionally engage with (the MC), which is an absolute must for any successful story. Try to look at this character objectively. They exhibit (traits that may not resonate with the viewers), all of which make it hard to really get behind this character. One solution would be to insert a moment early on in the script that shows this character during an instance of vulnerability, exhibiting a positive trait, being at a disadvantage, etc., to ensure that pivotal connection is made.
>
> Help the audience to emotionally connect with (the MC) by giving them a good reason to want to keep following them on their journey. At present, (the MC) is possibly just too (perfect/unlikable/unrelatable, etc.). Consider adding a 'save the cat' moment, showing a moment of vulnerability or by creating a relatable character flaw to not only make this character more realistic but to help add depth, too.

CHARACTER ARC

A character arc isn't an absolute necessary. In fact, certain genres don't particularly call for the hero to have changed along the way. Iconic characters such as Indiana Jones, Forrest Gump, and Ferris Bueller arguably didn't particularly change by the end of the movie, and sitcoms are literally based on the idea that it's the situation that changes every episode, not the characters, but having a MC learn something, grow, or show change throughout their journey can definitely generate more audience satisfaction as well as enhance the underlying central theme, so it's an additional factor what might just turn a good script into a great script.

Consider making a comment if;

THE MC HASN'T CHANGED BY THE END OF THE STORY

Again, to reiterate, this isn't an absolute rule. Not every character has to have changed or grown by the end of the script, but a writer can miss a great opportunity to create a rewarding story for the audience if their MC doesn't. This can easily occur during ensemble stories or scripts that contain dual protagonists, where not every character has been given enough screen time to have a satisfactory character arc, or in a short film, where there simply isn't enough time for any character development at all.

You can spot a fixed character by examining whether the central conflict was resolved or not, whether the protagonist overcame their character flaw, or if the MC continued to act in the same unconstructive manner that they did at the beginning. Point out to the writer that by not evoking any change in their protagonist, it could also cause other issues with their script. If there's no change in a character, it's also a clear indication that their journey has been too easy, that they weren't challenged enough, that there hasn't been enough conflict, or that turning points and story beats are weak.

Explain that a character doesn't have to change from negative to positive. You can still have a rewarding story about a nice guy who turns bad, and equally, if the writer is clear that the MC shouldn't show change by the end, then encourage them to have a moment in the story that at least gives the character the option to change in order to add a bit more depth. Ultimately, a clear character arc helps the audience to like, understand, and empathize with a character on a deeper level, so if there isn't any, advise the writer to reconsider adding some in.

CHEATS

What's not coming across quite as clearly as it could be is what lesson (the MC) has learned or how they've changed by the end of their journey. This isn't an absolute must in a story, but by not showing any character development, a great opportunity to create a more rewarding experience for the viewers is being missed.

Arguably, (the MC) is the same person at the end of the story as they were at the beginning, and this lack of character arc risks creating an unsatisfying ending for the viewers. Adding some significant change would help improve this. Or create a life-learning moment for his character by examining who they are at the end, then reverse engineering that, so that they're nothing like this at the beginning of the story or vice versa.

CHARACTER ARCS AREN'T BELIEVABLE

If a character suddenly goes from upstanding citizen to cold-hearted murderer in the blink of an eye, the audience will find it rather hard to swallow, meaning that sudden change without explanation can kill the believability of a character, a plot, or the entire movie. A writer needs to fill in the blanks and show the viewers exactly what motivates certain actions from certain characters, plus showing progression is also a great way to heighten story beats and turning points.

Anything that causes the audience to say "that would never happen in real life" or makes them stop to question logic usually isn't a good thing. Explain to the writer that an abrupt character transformation may risk coming across as unbelievable, questionable, and needs more exposition to justify it. If there are no clear motivations or reasons behind a character's growth or change, will the audience believe it?

CHEATS

More explanation as to why (character) decides to (take implausible action) is needed as it's hard to understand what's motivating this action, making it feel unbelievable. Either do more to set up this moment earlier on, provide a reasonable explanation after the event, or change the action to be much more in tune with how the viewers expect this character to react.

Be careful not to lose the audience's investment in the story by having an (unbelievable/implausible/improbable, etc.) character arc for (the MC). When (the MC) suddenly (goes off in an unexpected direction/does a one-eighty/changes their mind, etc.), because this wasn't set up properly, the audience may not swallow it.

Make sure that the transformation from (the MC's initial outlook) to (the MC's new outlook) is believable, otherwise, there's the risk of either confusing the audience or leaving them feeling cheated, neither of which is good. When (example from the script) occurs, it doesn't fit with the fact that (opposing example from the script), so make sure to ease into this transition by setting it up properly first.

THE MC DOESN'T HAVE ENOUGH ACTOR BAIT

If a character is mediocre, boring, or stale, it'll be hard to attract talent to play the part. Actors want to play challenging roles, become iconic characters, and work on projects that excite them just as much as we want to read and watch these characters on screen. Getting talent attached can be a great way to help sell a script, and with more and more actors creating their own production companies and actively looking for roles they'd love to play, regardless of whether it's a high concept or high budget production, a writer looking to promote their script absolutely needs their story to contain characters with not only Oscar winning potential, but that A-list stars can connect to on a personal level too.

How do they do that? By opening on big dramatic moments, crafting compelling dialogue, having strong psychological themes, giving us something new, having heightened conflict, writing a page-turning script, and creating demanding roles to play aka not playing it safe. If a writer doesn't have these things, do they really have a sellable project?

CHEATS
It's worth considering how appealing the role of (the MC) is going to be to talent. Having a role that top actors will be desperate to play can help take a script a long way, so consider heightening the drama, the conflict, and the emotional turning points in this character's story to help make the part that much more attractive to play.
Heightening the emotional turmoil for the protagonist would make this part much more appealing to play. Top talent want to take on challenging roles, but at present, is (the MC) facing enough difficult obstacles, decisions, or confrontations to entice actors to play this part?

ANTAGONISTIC FORCE

Screenplays don't always need to have a physical antagonistic character either, as an antagonistic force can be anything from an event, nature, time, inner emotions, a physical limitation, or even a miscommunication between characters, but the reason they're pivotal pieces in a story, is that they help to create more conflict. Antagonistic forces create an added obstacle that the protagonist must overcome, forcing them to rise to the occasion or face failure.

Consider making a comment if;

THERE IS NO ANTAGONISTIC CHARACTER

As mentioned, a story doesn't always require the antagonistic force to be a physical embodiment of a character as you can have anything from a major disaster to the protagonist being their own worst enemy each creating obstacles during the MC's journey, but that doesn't mean there's isn't room to include a minor antagonistic character in there too. The protagonist can't argue with a viral disease or an avalanche, so having a human (or humanoid) character for the MC to face off against can be a great way to explore theme, create explosive dialogue, generate a moment of victory for the MC, and its great actor bait too.

If the script lacks a villain because there's a larger antagonistic force for the protagonist to battle against, but there's also a lack of emotionally engaging content, ask the writer to consider using some of the minor characters to take on the role. By being directly at odds with the hero's decisions, goals, or attitude, a minor character could help introduce some poignant and memorable moments. Finding whichever secondary character has the weakest relationship with the MC is a good starting point.

CHEATS
Having a worthy opponent for the hero to fight is not only a great way to push the protagonist to the limits, it's a great way to create more conflict too, so seriously consider developing an antagonistic character to help do this.
There's a great cast of likable characters here that the viewers will certainly want to root for, but don't forget about creating an (antagonist/rival/nemesis, etc.) character too. Antagonists are great at adding more (conflict, rivalry, stakes, etc.), plus the audience loves a character that they can hate, so would it be worth including one in this piece too?

> **CHEATS CONT.**
>
> While (the MC) is clearly (their own worst enemy/up against a non-human antagonistic force), the audience also loves a character they can hate, so it's also worth considering creating an antagonistic character for the MC to fight against too.

THE ANTAGONIST ISN'T DEVELOPED ENOUGH

When an antagonist has been underdeveloped, it'll seem like they've only been inserted into the script to just obstruct the MC, leaving them feeling like a one-dimensional stereotype, which will ultimately leave audiences unsatisfied. No character is pure evil or all-good, and just like the protagonist, an antagonist needs to be believable, have depth, and be emotionally complex.

Encourage writers to devote the same amount of time to developing their antagonist as they did for their protagonist. An easy tip is to assume that the villain probably considers themselves as the hero of their own movie, with their own goals, emotional needs, stakes, flaws, and character arcs. Not every antagonist needs an extensive backstory, but the audience does need to understand why achieving their goal is so important to them in order to generate empathy or understanding for the character.

> **CHEATS**
>
> (the antagonist) feels slightly underdeveloped. We don't really know (much about this character/what's motivating them/why winning is so important to them, etc.) and this risks them coming across as one-dimensional. Flesh out this character just as much as the protagonist in order to add depth to the overall story.
>
> There's the risk that the antagonist is coming across as slightly too (cartoonish/pantomime villain/stereotypical, etc.), meaning that they lack depth and feel one-dimensional. (use examples from the script to help highlight this). But (the antagonist) has the potential to be so much more. Develop this character further, adding depth, relatable flaws, or even a sympathetic backstory to help make them become more engaging.

THE ANTAGONIST LACKS ENOUGH SCREEN TIME

This is a judgment call and a juggling act. Some of the most memorable villains in movie history, such as *Darth Vader*, *The Wicked Witch of the West*, or even *Jaws*, had very little screen time, yet they're still iconic characters. Sometimes withholding the reveal of the antagonist until the end of the story is necessary, and obviously, a writer should avoid allowing the villain to overshadow their protagonist during the story. But sometimes, a lack of setups or interaction with the MC can leave a screenplay feeling as though it's missing something.

You'll need to assess whether a script would improve if we saw more of the antagonist here. If there isn't enough backstory or development given to the antagonist, is it hard to understand what their motivations are in stopping the MC? Is the writer missing the opportunity to create more conflict, emotional turmoil, and tension by not including the antagonist enough? Should we see more reactions from the villain after minor wins or failures? Does the surprise reveal of the antagonist create more questions than it answers? Is the story missing an antagonist altogether, etc.?

CHEATS

At present, (the antagonist) feels rather under-used in this story. There's a really (interesting/engaging/unusual, etc.) character in (the antagonist) here, but they're not getting a whole lot of screen time. Is it worth giving the audience a little more of this potentially great cinematic character?

While (antagonist's name) works great when battling against (the MC) during the climactic third act, there's been a missed opportunity to make that moment more challenging for (the MC) by allowing us to see more of (the antagonist) throughout the rest of the story.

Do we possibly need a stronger sense of how (dangerous/challenging/powerful, etc.) the antagonist is here? At present, (the antagonist) only features a minimal amount throughout the script, making it hard to get a proper sense of the threat this character really poses.

THE ANTAGONIST IS A WEAK RIVAL

If the protagonist is easily beating their rival, overcoming obstacles without difficulty, or outsmarting the villain too much, then it won't feel as though they've struggled enough to fully deserve their reward at the end. Equally, if the antagonist only creates one obstacle as opposed to a series of increasingly difficult ones, the result will be the same. The antagonist needs to be an equal, if not stronger, adversary to the MC. If they're no real threat, then they're not being an effective opponent. The hero needs to be genuinely challenged in some manner by the antagonist in order to for them to be forced into changing or growing.

Antagonists should drive change in the MC and they work best when they're in direct opposition to the hero. Villains are often a 'dark reflection' of the protagonist, sharing similar character traits. Mirroring the protagonist and antagonist can work well to show character change if the MC experiences a moment where they realize that if they don't take another path, they might just end up turning into the villain.

If you feel the antagonist isn't being an effective rival for the MC, advise that the writer address this issue by letting the villain win more. If the antagonist always fails when trying to obstruct the MC, will the audience really believe that they're much of a threat when they turn up in the climactic scene to try again? Small victories along the way could help to make the antagonist appear stronger, and this also helps to up the stakes and increase the tension along the way too.

Writers can also enhance their antagonists by making them unscrupulous. If we truly believe they'll stop at nothing to get what they want, they'll instantly become a worthy opponent. Clearly defining the villain's motivations, telling us what they have to lose if they fail, and having them make difficult decisions, all go a long way to create believable and determined antagonists for the MC to battle against.

CHEATS

At present (the antagonist) isn't quite being the force to be reckoned with that they should be. The more challenging the obstacles the hero has to face, the more rewarding the story will be, but everything that (antagonist) throws at (the MC) seems to be easily overcome, which is means they're not much of a rival here.

> **CHEATS CONT.**
>
> A hero is only as great as their rival, meaning that the harder it is to beat (the antagonist), the greater the sense of achievement there will be for (the MC). Don't skip out on making the antagonist as (challenging/ruthless/strong-willed, etc.) as possible in order to elevate (the MC's) achievements at the end. At present, (the antagonist) isn't quite the rival they have the potential to be.
>
> Part of watching the protagonist grow is also watching them fail, but at present, we're seeing (the antagonist) fail slightly more often than (the MC), who easily overcomes the challenges, complications, and disruptions they cause. Creating more instances where (the antagonist) is allowed to win more often could help make them a much stronger adversary.

SUPPORTING CHARACTERS

Supporting characters can help to fill out the story world, they can either help or hinder the protagonist's progress, and they can also add to the drama, conflict, contrast, or humor of a piece too. Although the story isn't focused on them, secondary characters need to serve a purpose, whether that's exploring the theme, generating atmosphere, creating relationships with the MC, or playing pivotal pieces in the plot. Remember, the bigger the cast, the bigger the budget will need to be, so if a script contains minor characters that aren't adding to the story in any significant way, they become possible cuts.

Consider making a comment if;

SECONDARY CHARACTERS OVERSHADOW THE MC

It's not uncommon for side characters to become fan favorites, whether in fiction or film, as they often play very likeable roles, such as the comic relief, the loyal best friend, the quirky one, or the antagonist, who can be both charming and ruthless, but because we're technically not rooting for them, it doesn't matter if their lovable qualities are offset by their bad ones. Side characters also often get the best witty one-liners, they can say the things that the MC wishes they could say but can't get away with, and they can risk offending the audience a lot more, because they're not the focus of the story, but sometimes the writer has possibly overlooked the fact that one of their secondary characters might be more appealing than their protagonist, and this means that they're either writing the wrong person's story, or they need to give more attention to the hero.

This is really only something you'll be able to gauge yourself, but if you find you're more drawn towards a lesser character, you'll need to ask yourself why. Does a secondary character have more conflict in their plot thread? Are they saving the day or solving problems instead of the MC? Are scenes being told from a minor character's perspective, etc.?

It's perfectly fine to enjoy a minor, more memorable character, but if the true reason behind this is because the protagonist is boring, predictable, and too perfect, the problem isn't with the minor character, it's with the MC, so advise the writer that they've either chosen the wrong person to lead the story, or they need to do more to develop the MC into someone more worthy of following.

> **CHEATS**
>
> (secondary character) makes a great character, they're (positive remarks about the character), and audiences will warm to them immediately. In comparison, (the MC) is (negative remarks about the character), making them hard to (relate to/like/empathize with, etc.) at times begging the question, is the story focusing on the wrong character here?
>
> The ability to weave the various plot threads together in this piece is impressive, but be aware that there's (more conflict/a more satisfying character arc/more emotional drama, etc.) in (secondary character's) storyline than there currently is in (the MC's), begging the question, would (secondary character) make a more engaging protagonist than (the MC)? If the writer is determined that (the MC is the true hero here, then more work is needed to elevate their journey to make it as (exciting/engaging/interesting/dramatic, etc.) as that of (the secondary character).

SECONDARY CHARACTERS HAVE MORE SCREEN TIME THAN THE MC

A writer may struggle to keep the focus on their protagonist if we're seeing other characters more often than we're seeing the hero. This could be because they're trying to include too many story threads, or it might be because they're giving more prominence to a secondary character instead. If we're not seeing the MC as much as we should be because of the ensemble nature of the story, then it's important that when the MC does get screen time, they're present during the big turning points and emotional beats of the story. Structurally, the hero should feature in most of these beats, if not all of them, in order to give a clear indication that they are the primary thread. If this isn't happening, then the audience is going to get lost and be left uncertain of who they're really supposed to be following and why.

If we're seeing more of the love interest or side-kick on screen, similarly, there's going to be confusion as to who the actual protagonist of the story is. This could come down to a simple rookie error, where the writer introduced a minor character in the first scene of the script, duping the audience into thinking that they're the character they should follow, which is something to point out if you believe this to be the case, otherwise, hint to the writer that they're allowing minor characters to out-shine their MC, taking the attention away from them, and ultimately, distracting the audience from the true hero.

CHEATS

It can be difficult to juggle several plot threads, especially in an ensemble piece such as this, but it's important to ensure that there's more focus being given to the protagonist compared to the rest of the characters so that audiences understand whose story it really is. At present, that message is being muddled because (all plot threads are getting equal screen time/we're spending more screen time with the secondary characters than we are with the MC).

Make sure that (the MC) features in the major story beats during the script. As this is their story, those beats need to be focused on (the MC's) plot thread, as opposed to a secondary character. Take (example from the script) as an example. This is a great heightened emotional moment for (secondary character), but it's taking the attention away from (the MC), who is ultimately the star of the movie.

> **CHEATS CONT.**
>
> There could be some confusion as to who the protagonist of the piece is due to (secondary character) being introduced to us before (the MC).

SECONDARY CHARACTERS DON'T SERVE ANY REAL PURPOSE

There's no point in having characters that don't serve any real function. Secondary characters should either be helping, hindering, disrupting, or complicating the MC's path in some shape or form. If they're not, questions may need to be asked regarding why they're in the story.

It can become difficult to assess which minor characters are working and which aren't in pilot scripts, as a writer may have included a character that might feature more prominently in later episodes, yet doesn't play a significant role in the first. Without knowing the writer's intention, you can only highlight that said characters may be taking up pivotal screen time that might be better devoted to the main cast. Ask whether it might be worth saving the introduction of that minor character until a later episode, so as not to be throwing too many new faces at the viewers early on, to ensure that they'll not be forgotten, or whether the character can be cut or replaced by another reoccurring character instead.

If there's a secondary character without purpose, look to the traditional archetype roles for inspiration such as the mentor, the side-kick, the fool, the love interest, etc. Can any of them be applied to the character to help make them more active? Or could the writer be missing an opportunity to reflect on the central theme by using their secondary characters more effectively? Advise that a character risks being cut if they're not pivotal to the story, so suggest the writer use the character to create more conflict.

> **CHEATS**
>
> While (the MC) is (positive remarks), (secondary character) often comes across as just being a sounding board for (the MC) and doesn't really seem to add anything much to the plot. Consider giving this character a more archetypical role, such as the (mentor/the innocent/the jester, etc.) to make them serve more of a function within the plot, otherwise, they're another potential cut.
>
> With a cast this large, it's worth figuring out what function each of the supporting characters serve, especially within the protagonists' journey. At present, (efficient secondary characters) are working well as (whatever roles they play), but it's harder to see exactly what (inefficient secondary characters) are bringing to the table. Consider either cutting the number of characters used, condensing two or more into one role, or ensuring that each secondary is serving a pivotal role in the story.

SECONDARY CHARACTERS ARE ONE-DIMENSIONAL

This is a frequent problem in short scripts, where understandably, there's less time to spend on character development and where more often than not, the writer needs to quickly establish a certain character type without dedicating too much time to it. Stereotypes are immediately recognizable, therefore they cut down the time needed to introduce them to the audience, and while this can work well in certain genres, such as comedy, using one-dimensional characters can also come across as being a bit of a cheat as it shows that the writer perhaps doesn't have the skill to develop original characters. Stereotypes can often become offensive and they can become memorable distractions for all the wrong reasons.

In a longer format, stereotypes are more likely to creep into minor roles rather than secondary character roles, and if it's a character that we're only meeting once or twice for a short time, their inclusion becomes slightly more forgivable, however, if a character gets a significant amount of screen time, then it probably warrants a comment. Encourage the writer to step away from the stereotypes and to look for ways to create more diverse, believable, and relatable characters instead. It's worth spending just as much time when developing the supporting cast as on developing the MC.

> **CHEATS**
>
> (secondary character) is certainly your typical (stereotype/cliché), but using stock characters like this can risk coming across as a little bit of a cheat, which isn't helping to display the writer's true creativity. Consider adding more depth to this character to help make them more unique, more realistic, and more relatable.
>
> Cliched characters are flat characters who serve more as plot devices than engaging characters we want to follow, and at present, (secondary character) risks being described in this manner. The (cliché/stereotype) is a tired trope we've seen in this type of story for a long time now, so add more of a fresh take to this character if possible. What depth could be added to this character that would help them elevate them from (cliché/stereotype) to unique?

PASSIVE CHARACTERS

Passive or inactive characters can work when done well. Problem is, they're usually done badly. A passive character isn't driving the story forward, they're letting events happen around them while not making any decisions that advance the plot. Again, it can work well in various scenarios, such as when a character's purpose is to bear witness, like in *Forrest Gump* (1994), when they play victims such as Rosemary in *Rosemary's Baby* (1968), are being manipulated, such as Melanie Daniel's in *The Birds* (1963). Even the iconic Indiana Jones has been described as being passive. In *Raiders of the Lost Ark* (1981), he's simply reacting to events out with his control and a running joke is that if he hadn't been involved, the events would've ended up happening anyway, except for the delivery of the Ark at the end, that is, but more often than not, if an amateur writer has made their MC passive, it's probably left the story feeling boring and labored.

Consider making a comment if;

THE MC ISN'T SOLVING THEIR OWN PROBLEMS

A noticeable feature of a passive character is if they leave conflicts unresolved, are often being saved by others, or rely heavily on coincidence to solve their problems. While things like that can happen in a story, if it's overdone or executed during a pivotal story beat, it can result in the MC looking weak, pointless, or so incredibly lucky that audiences find it hard to swallow.

The viewers want to see the person they're following take action, save the day, fix the problems, etc. If a secondary character steps in and wins the climactic battle instead, the audience is going to feel a little let down that the hero they've been following didn't meet their expectations. If the MC doesn't have a hand in overcoming their own obstacles, there's every chance that the writer's making their journey far too easy for them, and again, that's scrimping on the amount of potential conflict they could include. The more the MC has to work to earn the reward at the end, the more satisfying it'll be to watch.

CHEATS

There's the risk that (the MC's) glory is being robbed by having (secondary character) swooping in at the very end to save the day. While this creates a rewarding ending for (the secondary character), shouldn't (the MC) be the one who achieves the goal they set out to attain at the beginning of the story?

Things have been made far too easy for (the MC) by having their problems solved by other characters (include examples from the script to highlight the point). It's much more rewarding for the audience to watch the protagonist overcome obstacles, and it's a great way to show character growth, so consider giving (the MC) more wins than they currently do.

Try to avoid creating a passive protagonist by allowing (the MC) to have more of a hand in (solving problems/succeeding/overcoming obstacles, etc.) rather than having these challenges overcome by secondary characters too often. If the hero isn't the one advancing the plot, the story is either focusing on the wrong character or it has a weak protagonist.

THE MC DOESN'T DRIVE CHANGE

Even when a character isn't in control of the events happening around them and maybe they don't even understand what's happening to them, they still need to be moving the story forward in some manner. This means they need to be making decisions (the harder the better) and taking action (even deciding not to take action is technically taking action) towards achieving whatever goal they may have. It's not enough for a protagonist to sit and passively observe what's happening in a scene and the audience can't see a character's thoughts and feelings unless they're shown. Advise any writer who isn't using their characters effectively to start doing so, otherwise, yet again, they're just going to end up boring the audience and the reader.

CHEATS

Because (the MC) is (letting other people make all the decisions/following other character's lead/ just going with the flow, etc.) they're being passive rather than active. Engaging protagonists are the ones who drive the story forward, make the tough choices, and take responsibility throughout the story, so it's well worth applying this to (the MC) as much as possible in order to avoid creating a character that the audience has difficulty rooting for.

(the MC) is at risk of being a passive character rather than an active one because they're letting other people (make the decisions/solve the problems/take action, etc.). Ensure that (the MC) isn't viewed as boring or in a poor light by the audience by having them be the one driving the story forward as much as possible.

Try to make (the MC) much more active than they currently are. As it stands, (examples of passivity from the script), meaning that (the MC) is a passive character, relying on others to (make decisions/drive the plot forward/solve their problems, etc.) Passive characters aren't interesting to watch, so the more (the MC) is at the helm of their own story, the more rewarding the piece will be.

DIALOGUE

Although there's great emphasis on showing, not telling, dialogue is an extremely important factor when delivering exposition, backstory, creating conflict, expressing tone, and moving the plot forward, but often, dialogue is only noticeable when it's really bad or really good, making it one of the most complicated screenwriting elements to make comments on. What you should look for in well-written dialogue is lots of subtext, memorable and powerful lines, a good pace, conflict, and efficiency. Less is almost always more when it comes to dialogue, so the quicker the character can get to the point, the better.

As usual, start with the positives and tell the writer what's currently working and why. Do voices carry consistently throughout? Are voices easily distinguished from one another? Does speech reflect the time period and setting well? Then dig deeper, using specific examples to highlight problem areas if you can.

Get used to recommending that writers do a pass where they read their dialogue out loud. This is a highly effective way of discovering lines that don't flow well when spoken, of finding repetitive wording and filler-dialogue, as well as being a great way to proofread at the same time, but few writers actively do this exercise, and it's easy to spot when.

CHEATS
The dialogue has been handled particularly well. It's naturalistic, believable, and evocative of the setting, meaning there's little to critique at this stage.
Dialogue is economic without any unnecessary talk occurring, isn't overly expository, is balanced well with the onscreen action, and contains lots of subtext, which is excellent.
Dialogue is a clear strength with the language being heavily evocative of the time period, location, and tone, yet it never feels overly foreign or alien, making it easily digestible for the viewers.

> **CHEATS CONT.**
>
> On the whole, dialogue has been written well, characters carry a consistent voice throughout, there's a clear differentiation between each character's voice, and speech feels appropriate to the time period and location.
>
> The dialogue is written extremely well with each character's speech expressing their diverse personalities, with distinct speech patterns, nuances, and where everyone's voice is also being carried consistently throughout.

EXPOSITION

What is exposition? It's all the information that the audience needs to know in order to follow the story. It's often delivered via dialogue, but on the whole, if a piece of info can be expressed visually, it usually creates a stronger impact, commonly referred to as 'showing, not telling', so there's definitely an art to delivering exposition without being too obvious about it. As with every scene, every line of dialogue needs to serve a distinct purpose. If it isn't, it's yet another potential cut.

Consider making a comment if;

THERE'S TOO MUCH DIALOGUE

This is a very common issue in early drafts where perhaps the writer has decided to get coverage notes far too early. Lengthy pages filled with dialogue tend to suggest that the writer's forgetting about the visuals and they're likely relying on dialogue to deliver exposition when they could easily be using action instead. Remind the writer that film is a visual medium and viewers will be paying more attention to what they can see than to what they can hear. What's going to be more interesting for the audience; hearing someone tell us how terrible someone is, or watching that person doing those terrible things on screen?

Ask the writer to be ruthless. If a line of dialogue isn't moving the plot forward, revealing character, is highly entertaining, or is giving us essential information, they probably don't need it. Also ask them to search for lines that could easily be replaced with an image and to consider if exchanging it for a reaction shot, an action, or even just a silence, would be more powerful for the audience.

Entering a scene late and leaving it early is also a great tactic to use. Greetings and goodbyes simply extend a scene longer than needed. They often prevent a scene from ending on the most powerful line possible and it hampers both the pace of the story and the read. Advise the writer jumps straight into the meat of the scene, makes the point, and then moves on, in order to keep things brief but powerful.

> **CHEATS**
>
> Don't forget that film is a visual medium and the viewers are going to be paying more attention to what they see on screen as opposed to the audio they hear, so attempt to tell the story using action and visuals slightly more than via speech alone if possible.
>
> This is a talky piece, and while there are some great lines in there, often it's taking too long to get to them or they're being (swamped/missed/overshadowed, etc.) by all the other unnecessary lines of dialogue on the page.
>
> At present, there's just too much dialogue, meaning that the story is being told to us rather than shown to us. 'Enter late and leave early', which means cutting the greetings and goodbyes, minimizing the filler chit-chat that isn't particularly moving the story forward, and ending on the most powerful line of the scene.
>
> This script is all dialogue with little action, and while that works great in a stage play, it's not quite enough to satisfy cinema-going audiences. Look for ways to deliver exposition visually if possible. This means showing the story unfold via action and imagery just as much as through dialogue. Consider what's going to be more interesting for the audience, listening to (example of heavy exposition from the script), or watching it unfold on screen?

DIALOGUE IS TOO ON-THE-NOSE

There's a time and a place for speaking directly, and in many instances saying exactly what's on a character's mind can work to great effect, but when character's frequently use on-the-nose dialogue, it can make them come across as unrealistic, fake, simple, and novelistic. Highlight that having too much on-the-nose dialogue can, in fact, be very helpful when it comes to the rewriting process. Now that it's clear what emotions the characters are expressing, it's easier to then begin to disguise that using subtext.

Dialogue becomes much more interesting (and realistic) when the audience is forced to read between the lines. People skirt around a subject. They'll say everything *but* the one thing they want to say. They tend not to point out the obvious. They use irony to deflect, etc., and this is what writers need to be making their characters do too. Advise the writer gets to grips with subtext and use it as much as they can.

> **CHEATS**
>
> Try to limit the amount of on-the-nose dialogue occurring throughout the script. These are the instances where characters are saying exactly what they think or feel, such as (examples from the script), but because people don't generally talk this way in real life, novelistic lines like this risk creating unrealistic characters. Use subtext to help disguise the true intentions behind a character's words whenever possible.
>
> There's a high frequency of on-the-nose dialogue occurring throughout the script, which often leaves both the characters and the story feeling unrealistic. Most people don't talk so bluntly in real life, so it can be jarring to have too many characters talking in this manner in a screenplay. On the positive side, now that it's clear exactly what characters want to say, it's easier to now figure out inventive ways to disguise that by using subtext.
>
> The on-the-nose dialogue risks the script reading more like a novel than a screenplay, so try to disguise a character's inner thoughts and feelings by using subtext. People don't just blurt out exactly what they're thinking. They skirt around the subject; they say everything but, they use irony, etc.

THERE'S TOO MUCH FILLER DIALOGUE

Chit-chat dialogue may make interactions between characters feel more natural, but movie characters rarely talk like people do in real life. There's a limited amount of screen time, and the writer's just wasting it by telling the audience info that doesn't really have much to do with anything else. This isn't to say that chit-chat dialogue can't work. If it's also advancing the plot, revealing character, creating conflict, expressing the theme, or delivering essential exposition, then no, there isn't an issue with using idle talk.

A script can get away with having one or two instances of filler dialogue if it's entertaining, a tension release, or helps to establish the setting. It can sometimes be hard to emulate dialogue for contemporary characters without adding the odd "um", "well," or "oh", but if it's obvious that it's being used to eke out the page count or if the writer thinks that letting their characters ramble continuously is making them more realistic, then it's worth making a comment. A good way to recognize whether dialogue is acting as a filler is if it's creating any conflict in the scene. If it isn't, ask the writer to question whether they really need it or not.

> **CHEATS**
>
> There's a fine line between writing realistic dialogue and having chit-chat dialogue that isn't moving the story forward. Be aware that too much filler dialogue can slow the pace of the story and get in the way of the good stuff.
>
> Try to limit any chit-chat dialogue that's essentially just space-filler on the page. If a line of dialogue isn't advancing the plot, delivering essential exposition, revealing character, or is entertaining, it doesn't need to be in a script. Lines such as (examples from the script) are great at creating naturalistic dialogue, but they're also slowing the pace of the story, the read, and if cut, wouldn't really hurt the scene.
>
> Try to minimize the filler dialogue. These are words such as (well, oh, um, just, etc.) or (chit-chat examples from the script), which can easily be removed without damaging the scene. In fact, cutting them will make scenes leaner and more effective. There's only a limited amount of time/space in a script, so every line has to move the story forward if possible.

THERE'S TOO MUCH Q&A DIALOGUE

Similar to chit-chat dialogue, this is when one character asks a question and another answers it, which sounds like a perfectly reasonable thing to do, but it can become a problem when a writer uses this back-and-forth Q&A which relentlessly goes nowhere.

> ALFRED
> I don't know how she gets away with it.
>
> SYLVESTER
> Gets away with what?
>
> ALFRED
> Inviting us to a party with no booze. You see that?
>
> SYLVESTER
> See what?
>
> ALFRED
> That fella's brought a hip-flask. You didn't see?
>
> SLYVESTER
> You mean that fella over there?

The repetitive nature of the conversation really slows the pace of the story. Good dialogue answers the question but skips the obvious answer to deliver new information, answering the question at the same time.

> ALFRED
> I don't know how she gets away with it.
>
> SYLVESTER
> She's a cheapskate. Fella over there's snuck his own booze in.

Ask the writer to look out for instances where Q&A dialogue risks frustrating the audience and encourage them to find more inventive and engaging ways to deliver exposition instead.

CHEATS

Try to limit the Q&A dialogue, such as (example from the script), where yes, the conversation feels realistic and natural, but the back-and-forth nature of the discussion hinders the pace, which risks losing the audience's attention.

> **CHEATS CONT.**
>
> Increase the pace by minimizing any Q&A dialogue which, although makes dialogue sound naturalistic, can get in the way of an unfolding plot. Take (scene from the script), where the back-and-forth dialogue not only creates a longer than necessary scene, a lot of lines are also repeating information we already know.
>
> There's some Q&A dialogue occurring that could be worth rewriting in order to help increase the pace, get to the point of a scene quicker, and make room for additional subtext. (scene from the

DIALOGUE REPEATS INFORMATION WE ALREADY KNOW

There's a difference between a reminder, foreshadowing, applying the 'Rule of Three', and repeating information just for the sake of it. Using dialogue to tell us something we already know, such as stating the obvious, is another example of space-filler speech, which also risks insulting the audience's intelligence. Examples of this are when characters describe what we can see on screen, meaning that they're probably re-stating the information already written in the scene heading or the scene description. Characters describing something we've already seen them do to another character or re-telling information that's already been delivered also comes under this umbrella. If it's a pivotal plot point that we need a reminder of, then yes, the line is being effective, but if it's not, it's not moving the story forward and is another potential cut.

Another instance is when characters say the same thing but in a different way, such as "I hate you", "you're a horrible person", "I can't even look at you", during the same conversation, again, they're not delivering any new information, so the plot isn't advancing. If there are any instances of this in the script, point them out to the writer and recommend they pick the strongest line and cut the rest. It'll create a more powerful scene and it'll also increase the pace.

> **CHEATS**
>
> Create a leaner script by limiting the repetition. (example from the script) is essentially the same as (repeated line), so pick the strongest one and lose the other. Any time the characters are repeating information we already know, it risks slowing the pace of the story, so do a pass searching for any instances that can be removed.
>
> Less is more when it comes to dialogue and any instances where a character is telling us something that we already know are potential cuts. Take (various examples from the script) as examples of unnecessary repetition that's slowing the pace of the story and making the script take longer to read.

WORDING IS REPETITIVE

We're not talking about speech patterns, mannerisms, or catch-phrases that can all help to create a unique and memorable character here, we're talking about reusing the same wording when it's clear the writer just wasn't imaginative enough to vary the language they were using, which can create a sloppy impression (this doesn't just apply to dialogue, but to the scene description too).

When a writer is using the same limited selection of words, the audience is quickly going to realize.

>   HARRY
>   He's talking rubbish.
>
>   PAUL
>   What are you talking about?
>
>   HARRY
>   I overheard him talking to Bob
>   about it.
>
>   PAUL
>   He can talk to whoever he wants
>   about it. I don't care who he talks
>   to.

It's a rather crude example, but you get the point. Characters who continually refer to others by name throughout the script is another example. Yes, someone's got to call a character by their name early on so the viewers can identify them (this is actually debatable), but people don't usually talk like this in real life, and it can quickly become tiresome (which is great if that's the effect the character is supposed to be creating, but not so much if we're supposed to like them instead).

Ask the writer to do a pass looking specifically for repetitive word usage and encourage them to be more imaginative and evocative with their vocabulary in order to keep the reader engaged.

> **CHEATS**
>
> In an early draft like this, don't worry, not everything needs to be perfect, but when it comes to the polishing stage, try to avoid repetitive wording. Take (page number or scene from the script), where the word (repeated word) is used up to (number of) times, which doesn't do much to express the writers wordsmanship.
>
> Readers are very attuned to spotting repetition in scripts, which can indicate an amateur writer, so do more to highlight both creativity and vocabulary by avoiding repeated words or phrases throughout the script. Take (example from the script), for instance, where the repetition risks lessening the energy of the scene.

THERE'S TOO MUCH TECHNICAL JARGON

There's a fine line between a writer displaying that they've done the research and know their story world inside out, and alienating the audience (and reader) with a barrage of unfamiliar words that they won't understand. Understandably, in some cases there's no escaping the use of industry-specific jargon, which is absolutely necessary to help convey realism, and thanks to television procedurals, many of those previously unidentifiable words are now common knowledge, but there is the risk that paragraphs filled with specialist wording will be skim-read, misunderstood, or easily forgotten.

The worst outcome is that the dialogue is going to bore the reader, so advise the writer to keep the tech-talk to a minimum and instead try to emphasize the emotion they're trying to convey during the scene, to compliment the dialogue with an engrossing visual that helps add sense to the lines being delivered, or better still, just use visuals to deliver exposition.

> **CHEATS**
>
> Be careful not to alienate the audience by being too heavy on the technical jargon. Understandably, the technical talk helps to give the piece a sense of authenticity, but if the majority of the audience doesn't understand what's being talked about for large portions of the story, then it feels rather detrimental and it's worth cutting back on or at least making things more easily digestible.
>
> It's clear that the writer has done their homework as the piece feels very well researched, but for those viewers who aren't as familiar with the subject matter, there are a few scenes that may leave them feeling bewildered, overwhelmed, or worse, bored. Consider limiting the technical jargon and using visuals to deliver exposition instead. Why have characters tell us something when it's more powerful to show us?
>
> There's a nice level of authenticity being added to the script thanks to the detailed technical talk, which adds to the realism. The problem is, it's not exactly entertaining to listen to, and may not translate well onto the big screen. Possibly limit the jargon to help enhance the emotional impact that's trying to be achieved alongside strong visuals to deliver this exposition rather than over relying on dialogue, making it more accessible to everyone.

VOICE

Writing realistic and compelling dialogue is almost an art in itself, but if a reader can't connect to a character because of a character's dialogue, it's a big enough factor on its own to prevent the script from moving any further forward. Simply put, bad dialogue will kill a script's chances. There are lots of different elements to consider when assessing dialogue, such as believability, authenticity, effectiveness, diversity, continuity, clarity, and tone, and novice writers will usually fall foul of making multiple mistakes early on it their career.

Consider making a comment if;

CHARACTERS SOUND TOO ALIKE

Sometimes the reason behind all the characters sounding alike is that they all share the writer's own voice, which is a common error for rookies, but this can also become a problem when a story is set during a period setting, an other-world setting, or in a regional setting, where it's difficult to escape the fact that the majority of the cast may talk with the same accents, colloquialisms, or pronunciations. Being able to tell one character from another by their dialogue alone really helps characters to come alive in the readers mind, prevents them from becoming confused with one another, and helps individualize the characters, so it's something that writers should be striving for.

Characters who use the same words when speaking, who mimic each other's slang, or use the same common phrases, risk blending in with one another, and this can become particularly noticeable when you have two characters who really ought to sound different. If you have a street-wise teenager talking in the same manner as a young toddler, or an elderly Asian grandfather reeling off the same lines as a Victorian cockney chamber maid, it will not come across as convincing or believable.

If voices are too similar, advise the writer to do more character development, add specific character traits to help make each one stand out, or individualize by introducing one or two key phrases that only that character uses. They need to figure out a way to make all of their major cast sound unique, memorable, but believable at the same time.

CHEATS

Understandably, if several of the characters are from the same (locale/background/culture, etc.) they're going to sound alike on the page, but it's important that each character is given a recognizable voice to prevent them from easily being confused with one another while reading.

A few of the characters tend to use the same phrasing, word choice, and speech patterns, such as (examples from the script), meaning that they all end up sounding the same. Not only does this stop them from being easily distinguished from one another, it shows a lack of creativity in the writing. Without going overboard, consider adding nuances, memorable catchphrases, ticks, slang, etc., to help give each character a unique voice if possible.

> **CHEATS CONT.**
>
> At this early stage, a lot of the characters may be guilty of taking in the writer's own voice rather than their own. A few of the characters use the same (phrasing/word choice/speech patterns, etc.), such as (examples from the script), which leaves them all sounding very much alike. Do more research on these characters if there's difficulty in making them sound authentic, but also consider adding accents, distinct tones, or memorable mannerisms to help voices become more unique.

DIALECTS AND ACCENTS ARE OVERUSED

Using brogues, mannerism, accents, or local pronunciations can certainly add flavor to a script, help establish the era and setting, and make individual characters stand out from one another, but overusing the device can also be overkill and it can seriously hamper the pace of the read as it can take longer to digest an unfamiliar word when reading.

I've read scripts that came with a glossary of terms at the end to help explain the many foreign words that the writer thought helped add an extra level of realism to the script, but the audience aren't going into a cinema with glossary, and readers don't have the time to sift back and forth in order to understand the dialogue being spoken, especially when it's not clear from the context of the scene.

Advise that yes, one or two instances used to good effect are welcome, but forcing the reader to work harder than necessary in order to figure out phonetically spelled words they're not familiar with should be avoided. It won't add to the enjoyment of the read.

> **CHEATS**
>
> Be careful not to overdo it with the (regional accents/dialects). While one or two instances certainly helps to add authenticity and bring the story to life, by using the device too often, it risks making the script harder to read, which is something to avoid at all costs.

> **CHEATS CONT.**
>
> Spelling words how they sound in order to make dialogue sound authentic works, and doesn't work, so be wary of doing this too often in this script. Anything that causes the reader to stop and re-read something is interrupting the flow and breaking the immersion into the story, so perhaps only use it during poignant moments rather than it being a frequent occurrence throughout.

DIALOGUE ISN'T REALISTIC

Having a high up political figure, an 18th century Russian Cossack, or even an alien life form living on another world talking street jargon with a New Jersey drawl may be stretching it a bit too far, meaning that unless established in the story world, audiences expect characters to talk and act within the realms of believability.

If English isn't a particular strength for the writer, it's not uncommon to see a lack of abbreviation being used, resulting in characters sounding robotic and unnatural. Other grammar faux pas include missing words, or writing them in the wrong order, resulting in confusion. Overusing exclamation marks or having too many words written in CAPS also risk it sounding like characters are shouting or over-reacting.

As always, recommend the writer do a pass where they read all of their dialogue out loud. This is great for finding words that may read well on the page but don't sound as good when verbalized, that jar when spoken, and to catch word structure that makes little sense, plus it's also a great way to proofread the script at the same time, so kills two birds with one stone.

> **CHEATS**
>
> Try to ensure that dialogue remains in keeping with the time period and setting. There are a couple of instances, such as (examples from the script), that feel too (modern/out of place/contemporary, etc.) for these characters to be saying, which risks creating a jarring moment for the viewers.

CHEATS CONT.

Dialogue is possibly the weakest element of the script, with lines often sounding too (robotic/unnatural/statement-like, etc.) Doing a pass reading all of the lines out loud can't be recommended enough here. Not only will this help find the lines that don't sound particularly realistic, it'll also help discover the ones that may well read well on the page, but don't flow as great when verbalized, plus it's a great way to proofread the script at the same time too.

PACE

Think of pace as the heartbeat of the movie. It's how fast or slow the story is moving and there are several factors that can alter the pace throughout. The length of a scene, the amount of scene description, the number of story threads, sentence structure, and how much dialogue there is can all contribute to the pacing of a story. Pace is important, as it can dictate the audience's attention. Too slow a pace and there's the risk that viewers will tune out and become disinterested. Too fast a pace and there might not be enough time for the audience to connect with the characters and the story can feel rushed and unfulfilling.

Amateur writers can certainly find it difficult to create, maintain, or even fully understand pace, as it's one of those tricky elements that's hard to convey, often resulting in this element being ignored. In reality, it's an extremely important factor when it comes to keeping the audience engaged, and definitely worth commenting on if a writer is struggling to master it.

CHEATS
The piece is well-paced with short and punchy scenes that help drive the story forward.
Much like the read, the pace is a quick one. Scenes are short; move quickly and succinctly, with a good balance between action and dialogue within them.
Scenes are engaging and the action is great at pulling the reader in. The description has been nicely broken up on the page and this helps pull focus on the essential elements as well as driving the dramatic momentum.
There's a great pace to this piece, which takes the reader on quite the emotional rollercoaster, with high tension and moments of light relief all occurring at just the right times.

DRAMATIC MOMENTUM

We've all seen the structure diagrams with the rising line that indicates the increasing conflict that should happen before dropping off after a major beat before rising again. Up and down, up and down, but what is dramatic momentum and how can you spot when it's missing in a screenplay?

In its simplest form, dramatic momentum is what creates a page-turning script. When the plot gets progressively more interesting, tense, or gripping, that's the drama being upped and the viewers' attention becomes focused. There's a small drop in intensity after every major plot point, allowing the audience to catch their breath and ready themselves for even more escalation, but placing a lull in the drama at the wrong time, too often, or not enough, can disrupt the flow, leaving an unsatisfying pace.

Consider making a comment if;

THERE ARE NOTICEABLE LULLS IN THE STORY

The lull after mid-point is a common occurrence when a writer has simply run out of steam after the 'fun and games' part of the second act, but controlling the pace throughout an entire script can be extremely difficult. If there are any moments during a read where your attention starts to wane, that's precisely when you need to take note and ask yourself just why that's happening.

If the script has been boring from the beginning, it's not so much of a pacing issue than a concept issue, in which case you may need to highlight to the writer that they need to do more to increase the hooks, up the conflict, and work to ensure that their story does more to grab the viewer by providing the unexpected, posing a gripping question, or creating a 'what happens next?' moment etc. Be encouraging. No one likes the 'it's not original enough' comment, so you need to be careful with your wording. The writer may have also started their story too early and have too much cumbersome setup that gets in the way of the good stuff, in which case, advise the writer gets into the meat of the story much sooner.

If there are noticeable lulls elsewhere, figure out if it's due to scenes being too long or because of scenes being altogether unnecessary. They're both common occurrences for novice writers and both are caused by overwriting. If the action or dialogue in a scene isn't moving the story forward, it's also killing the dramatic momentum, so you may need to advise that a writer either ensures that every scene is effectively doing this or that they need to remove the scene.

Every scene needs to be able to hold the audience's attention, so point out that it's not just pivotal to grab the reader from the first page. This needs to happen continually throughout too. Again, throw in reminders about getting to the point of the scene faster, limiting the 'fluff' in the description, and keeping what's just come before and what's coming next in mind when assessing how the writer wants the audience to feel when watching.

CHEATS

While the script does well to (positive comment) and has the potential to please its target audience, at the moment, there's just not enough happening in terms of conflict or drama to ensure that audiences will be kept sufficiently hooked throughout.

There's a noticeable lull in the (action/drama/pace, etc.) after (story beat) in the script, which runs the risk of losing the interest of the audience. Consider (suitable recommendation by the reader) to help inject more conflict and keep the dramatic momentum going here.

The script may have fallen foul of the common post-midpoint lull where there's a dip in the dramatic momentum. While it's fine to create breather moments in between tension-filled scenes, staying in that comedown too long risks losing the audience's attention. Add new conflicts, heighten old ones by upping the stakes, insert a dramatic reveal or compelling hook, etc., to make sure that the viewers remain engrossed at all times.

THERE ARE NO 'CATCH YOUR BREATH' MOMENTS

It's rare to find this in a spec script, and if anything, you're more likely going to be congratulating the writer for taking you on a whirlwind ride than chastising them for not giving you enough time to catch your breath, but on the off chance that you find a script that's constantly increasing the drama without a break, it may be worth writing a comment about it just so that the writer is aware and can prepare for any future development notes they may receive further down the line.

Make sure that you highlight that the consistent fast pacing is to be applauded. Hopefully, that made the script a quick read, and you were engaged the entire time (although anything at a consistent pace, no matter what the speed, can become tedious). Ask the writer to consider finding a place in the script to take a break from the high-octane pace and to use it to pull focus on character development. It's usually in the aftermath of defeat or in the downtime after a big conflict that characters get time to prepare another plan or to do a little self-reflection aka growing.

Recovery scenes are great places to explore character relationships, inner thoughts, feelings, memories, and realizations, which are just as important to have in a story as the action is. Explain to the writer that they may be missing the opportunity to include these rewarding moments for the audience if they don't take a breather at some point during the story.

CHEATS

The writer has done an excellent job of delivering a high-paced action-packed story, making this a great genre piece, but don't forget to create a couple of moments that allow the audience to catch their breath in between the relentless drama too.

In terms of pacing, the audience is going to be on the edge of their seats the whole way through, which is an impressive achievement, but be aware that this relentless tempo doesn't leave much room for any character development, which is certainly worth considering creating in order to add more depth to the piece too.

The pace of the story is incredible, making this a quick and compelling read, but the writer has also possibly forgotten to add some catch-your-breath moments for the viewers (and characters) along the way too. The recovery between action sequences, the downtime when developing a new plan, and the rallying after a loss moments are great places to add character development, which will help elevate this piece even further.

REPETITION OF INFO HAMPERS THE PACE OF STORY

Be careful not to confuse repetition for reminders here. Repeating pivotal info can and does have value, especially when there are a lot of other things happening in the plot and the viewers may have missed a moment of foreshadowing earlier in the story. What we're talking about here is crowding the page with unnecessary details which make the script take longer to read (who wants that, right?) and can also run the risk of insulting the audience's intelligence at the same time too.

A writer doesn't need to list every single item in a room to paint an effective picture, for instance. Often a well-worded scene heading can be enough. Similarly, stating the obvious is just wasting words on the page. "he holds the gun in his hand", "looks with her eyes", "sits down" etc., are all common examples. Repeating information in dialogue can hamper the pace just as badly if characters are verbalizing what the audience can literally already see on the screen or when delivering the same exposition to multiple characters.

Depending on which elements are being repeated in the script, remind the writer of the "less is more" mantra, which can be applied to description, dialogue, and almost every other aspect of screenwriting. Detail the advantages of cutting things back to the core; a faster read, a more focused plot, more impressive wording, etc. Ultimately, repetition slows the pace, and that's something a writer should try to avoid as it could mean boring the viewers (and the reader).

CHEATS

Be careful not to waste time by repeating info that's already been given. Take (example from the script), which is already (implied/indicated/hinted at, etc.) by (correlating example), meaning we're just learning the same thing twice. Repetition like this slows the story and the read, so do a pass and eliminate all other instances.

Help tidy up the script and make it leaner by eliminating any instances where information is being unnecessarily repeated. Take (example from the script), which are already (implied/indicated/hinted at, etc.) by (correlating example), making them potential cuts.

THERE'S A LACK OF WHITE SPACE ON THE PAGE

The more white space there is on the page, the more appealing the script will look and the quicker it can be read. Time equals money in this business, so the faster you can read a screenplay, the more money you can earn, so readers naturally loathe any script that takes them longer than necessary to get through. Advise writers to de-clutter their script in order to improve the pace of the read and the story. This can work well with screenplays that are on the short side, but there is a risk of increasing the page count by doing this, so it may be a case that this applies more to action sequences or high-impact emotional scenes only.

Remind the writer to avoid writing paragraphs that take up any more than five lines on the page, but take it further by advising that they consider breaking up their description into even smaller segments by imagining that every new shot on the screen warrants a new line on the page. This can be great at highlighting specific emotions, reactions, actions, or props that might otherwise be skim read or missed while inside a much larger chunk of text.

This can also apply to dialogue, where any lengthy paragraphs may benefit from being broken up by inserting a visual. All too often, a writer gets caught up in delivering the dialogue and forgets that they need to keep the audience's eyes busy at the same time. Static shots without movement can become boring after a while, plus film is a visual medium more than an audio one, so injecting an image, a reaction, or action can help with this.

Feel free to divulge exactly why text-heavy pages are off-putting to industry readers, but also express why breaking up things on the page can help pull focus on the important details in a story at the same time as highlighting any possible word cuts that are crowding the page.

CHEATS

The faster the read, the more the reader will appreciate the effort, and as readers are the first hurdle a script needs to get over, doing everything possible to make the read a quick and enjoyable experience can go a long way, so avoid large blocks of text on the page if possible.
Breaking up large blocks of text on the page will make the script look much more appealing and it'll help increase the pace of both the read and the story.
Consider creating more white space on the page by placing every new shot on the screen on a new line on the page and inserting a reaction shot, an action, or image to help keep the viewer's eyes busy during lengthy monologues. This is a great way to prevent pivotal info from being lost or overlooked and it'll help make the script much faster to read too.

READABILITY

One of the first assessments a reader makes, is the level of professionalism that a script is at, and this goes a long way to informing them of the overall skill level that the writer has too, making readability one of the most important and yet often underestimated areas to comment on. While concept is key, the readability of a script can really make or break a script's ability to sell, and often writers can be guilty of forgetting that their screenplay needs to be as entertaining and engaging to read as it will be to watch.

Don't fall into the trap of reeling off formatting error after formatting error here. You're not proofreading or editing the script, so instead focus on the one or two areas that the writer needs to significantly improve on that are hindering the script's chances of selling. As usual, begin with praise. Does the script look professionally laid out? Does it adhere to the industry standard format? Was it a quick and engrossing read with lots of white space on the page, etc.?

CHEATS
Overall, the writing is engaging, evocative, and lean, making this a quick read but also an enjoyable one, which makes it a rare find indeed.
The script is written professionally, the formatting adheres to industry standards, and there's plenty of white space on the page, making this a quick read.
The excellent writing is by far the selling point of this script.
There's a gripping first page that sets the tone extremely well.

TITLE PAGE

It's unlikely that you'll ever need to make a comment regarding the title page, as this is the least important aspect when writing coverage. That said, there's still value in warning a writer if they've made some questionable errors, but this isn't something to spend a lot of time discussing and is really more of a side note to add towards the end of a section or in the conclusion, if at all.

Consider making a comment if;

THERE IS NO TITLE PAGE

Having no title page attached could've been a simple mistake that was made when creating the .pdf file, but a gentle reminder may be needed if the writer forgot to attach one to their screenplay, although if you have to mark the title and author both as being 'Unknown' or 'N/A' on your script report because you didn't have access to the information because of this, then it's fairly obvious, and you probably don't need to mention any further.

If the script wasn't very good, it's probably just as well that the writer didn't include their details, as there's no value in flashing your name around town if all it does is conjure up memories of reading a bad script, but regardless of the quality of the writing, it's still good practice to make sure a title page with all the correct information is included on the off-chance that the script is good enough to draw attention to it, in which case, the writer is only making it more difficult for any interested party to get in touch with them.

> **CHEATS**
>
> While some contests require that a title page or contact details be removed from submissions, it's good practice to ensure that any script you send into the industry has one.
>
> Make sure to attach a title page with all the correct details, including the writers name and contact details. It's much easier to find them at the beginning of a script than it is to search through countless emails to find this information, which is almost always needed by whoever is reading it.

CONTACT DETAILS ARE MISSING

What's just as bad as having no title page at all is having one that doesn't include vital information, such as the author's name or contact details. Reiterate the importance of including this information firstly on the basis that neglecting to do so risks making the writer look amateur or worse, careless, creating a bad first impression, and secondly, if their screenplay ends up impressing the reader, by not having these pivotal details immediately to hand, there's the chance that the original email has been lost and the reader might not risk passing the script onto interested parties because of this. Basically, the writer isn't doing themselves any favors by omitting this information.

CHEATS

On a side note, (positive comment about the script), it's well worth including contact details on the title page. If there's interest in a script, it's essential that it's made easy for someone to get in touch with the writer.

Make sure contact details are also listed on the title page. Don't make it unnecessarily hard to get back in touch, just in case someone falls in love with the script.

Accidents happen, so on the off chance that the original email is accidentally deleted or lost in amongst hundreds of others, make sure to list contact details on the title page too.

THE TITLE PAGE HAS UNNECESSARY ELEMENTS

To reiterate, it's more valuable to the writer for your notes to concentrate on the major issues that need addressed with the writing than it is to pinpoint small annoyances, and, yes, while it isn't recommended in the slightest, it is sometimes nice to see a title page that's tried to be a bit more creative than is required, so this isn't really something that you'll comment on unless the additions are so off-putting or inappropriate that it isn't doing the script any favors.

If you have to, remind the writer that, as with anything that stands out from the norm when it comes to screenplay layout, there's more chance of irritating the reader than there is of impressing them here, so play it safe. Stick to only using courier 12pt font and get rid of any distracting imagery, because if a writer needs to rely on visuals to sell their script, it gives the impression that perhaps the words aren't strong enough on their own. Title pages also shouldn't include the logline, any personal notes to the reader, and arguably, even including the WGA registration number, is sometimes seen as the mark of an amateur writer.

> **CHEATS**
>
> Avoid creating an immediate negative impression by removing (elements) from the title page.
>
> While the (images/fancy fonts/large text, etc.) are certainly eye-catching and creative, no reader has ever complained of a plain regularly formatted title page. It's better to be safe than sorry, so avoid any potentially negative impressions by trying to stand out.
>
> Be aware that including (images/fancy fonts/large text, etc.) on the title page usually just screams 'amateur writer', so it's well-worth avoiding creating this impression by playing it safe and having a regularly formatted page instead.

FORMATTING

With freely available screenwriting software and access to a trove of downloadable screenplays online, there's few excuses left for having a poorly formatted screenplay. A badly formatted script highly suggests that the writer has probably never even read a real screenplay, and as this is one of the most fundamental ways to learn the craft, it won't do much to convince a reader that a writer is serious about their career.

While it can be very tempting to let notes regarding poor formatting take up tons of space in your report, and again, this depends on the number of pages you need to fill, try not to get bogged down in listing every single formatting error that writers make. Sure, you can highlight one or two specifics that help highlight a point, but try to make a more general statement about which areas need work and advise the writer reads other screenplays, where they'll ultimately learn how to format their script properly as well as how to craft an engaging story, hook the reader, create tension… the list goes on!

Consider making a comment if;

STANDARD INDUSTRY LAYOUT IS INCORRECT

If a writer hasn't gone to the effort of presenting their script in the expected manner, then why would a reader go to the effort of considering it? But in certain circumstances, whether it's a lack of finances, a lack of recourses, or a lack of education, then yes, there are going to be newbie writers out there who've been unable to present their script in the correct format, so have compassion, don't dwell too long on the point, but do mention any free and accessible solutions you think would benefit them.

If you're used to reading scripts regularly, the small cheats that writers sometimes use will stick out like sore thumbs. Altering the page margins, the line spacing, or the font size are all crafty ways of cutting the length of screenplay, but they're all also very obvious, so advise the writer uses other methods to achieve the same effect, such as a harsh edit that removes any fluff, cutting any unnecessary word use, minimizing the cast, and condensing locations.

If a writer used the header and footer to relay title and author name on each page, for example, advise that this clutters the page unnecessarily and risks distracting the eye. Also recommend that any images or unusual fonts being used within the script be removed, as these things will only make a script stand out for the wrong reasons. It's not uncommon to see a script include scene numbers (which makes the script come across as being unfinished), and although it's recommended these be removed before submitting the script elsewhere, their inclusion may be of some benefit when you need to direct a comment to a specific point during your report, so it's not really something you need to spend time highlighting.

CHEATS

Any writer who wants to be taken seriously needs to get to grips with screenplay formatting. Consider investing in screenwriting software, which will allow more focus to be placed on the writing the story instead of the presentation.

It's very clear from the layout of the script that the writer is very new to screenwriting. One of the best ways to learn about formatting is by reading other spec screenplays. There are plenty of freely available screenplays online, which can really help writers get to grips with what a professional script has to look like.

Poor formatting is an instant giveaway that the writer lacks experience, but there's an easy fix that will help here. Read other screenplays. It's one of the best ways to get to grips with exactly how a professional screenplay should look, as well as what makes a gripping story and what doesn't.

THERE ARE TOO MANY FORMATTING ERRORS

Nothing gives away a writer's lack of experience more than a script riddled with formatting errors. For anyone first attempting to write a screenplay, the difference in layout from a standard novel can be daunting, and this is really only something that can be fixed by either finding a decent formatting guide to go by or by reading other screenplays. Try to avoid highlighting every single little instance or error here, but certainly give one or two examples in cases where it would clearly benefit the writer to understand where they're going wrong.

There are so many areas where a writer can make a formatting mistake. Is the information in the scene header correct and in the right order? Is CONTINUOUS being confused with SAME TIME? Does the writer frequently use unnecessary transitions such as CUT TO:, DISSOLVE TO:, or WIPE TO:? Are flashbacks, montages, and dream sequences properly formatted? Is the writer using dual dialogue when they shouldn't be? Are parentheticals being used correctly and placed in the right place? Are character names only written in capital letters when first introduced, etc.? Make sure that you're well versed in what's correct and what isn't before making comments.

CHEATS

Numerous formatting errors quickly reveal the writer's lack of experience. Thankfully, there's an easy fix. Reading other spec screenplays is one of the best ways to get to grips with formatting, plus it's a great way to discover what makes a page-turning script and what doesn't, so this cannot be recommended enough.

Getting to grips with formatting is a must if this script is to compete with thousands of others. This is an essential requirement, not an additional extra, so grab a formatting reference book, or better still, read more spec scripts, which is by far the best way to not just improve formatting, but screenwriting as a whole too.

There are a few formatting errors, such as (specific examples from the script and how to correct them), that need to be tidied up in order to give this script the best chance possible.

SCENE HEADINGS ARE CONFUSING

When caught up in trying to deliver the story they're excited about, amateur writers can be guilty of forgetting about the fundamental basics such as placing a scene INT. or EXT., confusing the meaning of CONTINUOUS for LATER or SAME TIME, or not beginning a new scene when the location has clearly changed.

If a writer is missing specific information that's making the story hard to follow, they're going to be interrupting the flow of the read, as a reader may stop to question logic, which is definitely something to avoid. You don't need to spend a lot of time detailing why each error needs to be rectified, but do suggest that the writer double checks their scene headings are consistent and correct in a final polish, that they brush up on how to format a screenplay if required, or go back and read more screenplays to help them get to grips with writing them.

CHEATS
There are a couple of slipups being made when writing scene headings, which risk revealing the writer's inexperience, so getting to grips with correct formatting is something to work on here.
Be careful not to confuse (CONTINUED/SAME TIME/LATER, etc.) for (correction) during the script. (explain the correct way to use whatever the primary problem is)
Avoid creating confusion by doing a pass to ensure that none of the scene headings are misleading. (point out specific errors from the script) Remember, any time a reader has to stop in order to question logic, the immersion into the story has been broken, so make sure that everything is as clear on the page as possible.

PARENTHETICALS

While you'll see them used more frequently in TV scripts than in features, parentheticals tend to be overused by amateur writers who want to make sure that absolutely every instruction is perfectly clear. When used well, the device can be an efficient and useful tool, but used incorrectly, they can quickly start to hamper the flow of the read, take up way too much space on the page, and they risk patronizing the reader too when they're used to state the obvious.

Consider making a comment if;

PARENTHETICALS ARE USED UNNECESSARILY

Parentheticals are helpful when the meaning of a line could be easily misunderstood, such as when someone's being sarcastic, but if a writer has used them when the emotion or intent is obvious, then they're just wasting space on the page.

Point out that a parenthetical takes up a whole line on the page to itself, so the writer needs to be extremely sure that they need it. Using them to direct speech to a specific character, such as `(to James)` or to add context to a situation, such as `(without looking up)` is fine, but if the writer is over-directing the actor with things such as `(sighs)`, `(furrowing his brow)`, or `(licking her lips)`, advise that actors, whose job is to bring characters to life, generally don't appreciate having every single action dictated to them in a script.

Similarly, if the writer is using parentheticals to direct action that should be written in the scene description, they need to be told otherwise, especially if a parenthetical is taking up two or more lines. Again, a few instances aren't going to be deal-breakers when selling a script, so only bring this to a writer's attention if they're over-relying on parentheticals to deliver the emotion, rather than using tone, context, action, or dialogue instead.

> ### CHEATS
>
> Do a pass looking for any unnecessary parentheticals being used. Very often, the dialogue, context, and tone of the scene is already strong enough, meaning that a line on the page is being wasted to tell us something that's already perfectly clear.
>
> Writers can get away with detailing small gestures or maneuvers in parentheticals, but in general, action should be placed in the scene description. A good rule of thumb to use is if an action is taking up more than one line in a parenthetical, it shouldn't be there.

> **CHEATS CONT.**
>
> Parentheticals are extremely useful if a line of dialogue could easily be misunderstood, but if the intention is fairly obvious, it's just wasting precious story-telling space on the page.

PARENTHETICALS ARE USED TOO OFTEN

There's nothing wrong with the occasional parenthetical. They can help inform us of the true meaning behind a line and they can also help define the tone too, but if there's any more than three separate uses on the same page and the rest of the script is also littered with them, then you may need to address that the writer is possibly relying on the device far too much. Also note that parentheticals should only be a handful of words long, so any action that's spanning over one line in length should be placed in the scene description, where it'll work better to break up the visuals from the dialogue.

Encourage the writer to strengthen the tone of a scene rather than insert a new parenthetical every other line to highlight an emotion. Ideally, the context of a scene and the strength of the dialogue should be enough to convey the intention behind a line, and more often than not, you'll be able to point out that the writing is already strong enough, so there isn't any real need for the writer to be using parentheticals, as they're not telling us anything we don't already know.

> **CHEATS**
>
> There's possibly an overreliance on parentheticals occurring throughout the script, when ideally the tone, the context, and the emotions of the scene should be strong enough to convey how a line should be delivered.
>
> Be careful not to overindulge when using parentheticals, which should be used sparingly and only when there's a strong chance that a line of dialogue could be misinterpreted.
>
> Using parentheticals too often can show weakness in a writer's ability to convey subtext and character intention.

PRESENTATION

If a screenplay doesn't look the part, it's not going to get very far. I've read scripts that were written in prose like a novel, PDF's of printed out pages that had been scanned, badly formatted word documents, scripts that didn't use the standard courier 12pt font, amongst a whole host of other drastic variations, and a lack of professionalism in the presentation only ever creates a negative impression. If a writer wants to be taken seriously, adhering to the industry standard layout isn't an optional requirement, it's a fundamental essential.

Consider making a comment if;

THERE ARE HUGE PARAGRAPHS OF TEXT

Large blocks of text, whether it's scene description or dialogue, is immediately off-putting to readers as it instantly tells them that the script is going to take longer than normal to read, and in this business, time means money. Advise against creating a negative first impression by suggesting the writer spaces out the wording in order to create more white space on the page, which will make the piece look more like a screenplay and less like a novel.

There's always the risk that a text-heavy script ends up being skim read, with vital pieces of information getting lost or missed, so ask the writer to do a pass cutting up any paragraphs that take up over five lines on the page. A helpful tip is to get the writer to think of each new shot on the screen as a new line on the page. This may mean that some lines only contain one or two words, but it encourages the writer to think visually at the same time as pulling focus on the important details in the story, making the writing punchier and increasing the pace.

CHEATS

Large blocks of text on the page immediately tell the reader that a script is going to take longer than usual to get through, and that can create a negative impression. Avoid this by breaking up the description into paragraphs no longer than five lines long.

> **CHEATS CONT.**
>
> Break up large blocks of text in order to create more white space on the page, which will help make the script look more appealing and increase the speed of the read.
>
> In order to increase the pace of the read, consider breaking up large paragraphs of text into smaller chunks. An easy way to do this is to give every new shot on the screen a new line on the page. This is a great way to help pull focus on the essential details and highlight ones that can potentially be cut too.
>
> Break up long paragraphs of dialogue on the page by inserting a visual to help increase the pace, to place more emphasis on the important pieces of exposition, and to keep the audiences' eyes busy during long-winded monologues.

THE SCRIPT HASN'T BEEN PROOFREAD

Even the best of us can be found guilty of having the occasional error that wasn't picked up during a proofread, so this isn't something to berate writers about. That said, if there are so many mistakes that it frequently interrupts the flow of the read, then yes, it's something that needs to be addressed.

Nevertheless, if a story is engaging, even bad spelling and grammar can become forgivable, but any errors that occur on the all-important first page can go an especially long way to creating a bad first impression, as it almost suggests that the writer has just been plain sloppy. Always point out that it's essential that the first ten-pages or so are as polished as humanly possible. If it's obvious that English isn't a first language, recommend that the writer use a proofreading service or even an editor to help them iron out any errors or inconsistencies that are causing confusion. And encourage the writer to do a pass where they read their screenplay out loud, not just the dialogue, which is a great way to catch any blunders in the wording, typos, character name mistakes, and poor punctuation.

> **CHEATS**
>
> Although the script is clearly still in development, at present, there are enough (spelling/grammatical/punctuation, etc.) errors occurring frequently enough throughout the script to interrupt the flow of the read.
>
> If English isn't the writer's first language, it's worth getting someone to proofread, especially before submitting it into contests or to producers, just to catch any errors that might hamper the enjoyability of the read.

SCENE HEADINGS ARE TOO LONG

Lengthy headings can be a sign that the writer lacks the ability to self-edit and ones that are long-winded or take up more than one line on the page don't look great, plus they're also fairly cumbersome to read. Unfortunately, headers are a necessary reminder that we're reading a screenplay, so it's to the writer's advantage to limit the amount that they break immersion into the story.

Being too specific isn't advised, such as:

```
EXT. NEW YORK - FIFTH AVENUE - PENTHOUSE SUITE - BALCONY
- NIGHT
INT. FOOTBALL STADIUM - FRONT ROW - MIDDLE SEAT - NIGHT
INT. NEWLY RENOVATED SANDSTONE GEORGIAN MANSION -
SERVANTS QUARTERS - DAY
```

There's a certain leeway that writers can use in order to shorten scene headings when writing sequences that don't change location.

```
INT. SKYNET HEADQUARTERS - HARRISON'S OFFICE - DAY
INT. SKYNET HEADQUARTERS - CORRIDOR - CONTINUOUS
INT. SKYNET HEADQUARTERS - LIFT - CONTINUOUS
```

All of which could easily be shortened to:

```
INT. HARRISON'S OFFICE - DAY
CORRRIDOR - CONTINUOUS
LIFT - CONTINUOUS
```

And in some cases, even the CONTINUOUS instruction can probably be cut.

If there isn't room to point out specific examples, usually a note regarding how shorter scene headings will improve the flow of the read is all that's needed.

CHEATS

Don't make a script take any longer than necessary to read. Trimming down lengthy scene headings is one way to help increase the pace of the read, so do a pass looking to keep things short, punchy, and to the point as much as possible.

Unnecessarily long scene headings risk hampering the pace of the read. Take (specific example) for instance, which could easily be shortened to (reader's suggestion) without losing any meaning.

A well-written script should immerse the reader into the story world, but excessively long scene headings risk breaking that engagement. They're unavoidable reminders that we're reading a screenplay, but that disruption can be minimized by keeping headings as short as possible.

BOLD OR CAPS HAVE BEEN OVERUSED

There's no real need for anything in a screenplay to be written in bold, although you may occasionally find that scene headings in TV scripts are written this way depending on the show format. Using bold is a stylistic choice, but it's not something that's going to score a writer any extra points. In fact, it's more likely to be distracting to the eye if they're overused. Writing elements in CAPS not only places extra strain on the eyes, it also risks the word being confused with character names or scene headings, so advise they both be used at the writer's own risk. Overusing bold or CAPS isn't a dealbreaker, but point out that they may be hampering the enjoyment of the read.

CHEATS

It's a stylistic choice for writers, but don't make the read any harder to get through than necessary. Bold or capitalized words put more strain on the eyes, so be mindful not to overuse them.

> **CHEATS CONT.**
>
> Using bold or capitalizing words for emphasis comes from stage plays where it was used to help highlight sound effects, but it's not necessary to highlight props, emotions, or actions, such as (examples from the script) in a screenplay. It's a stylistic choice, but you risk breaking the immersion into the story by shouting words at the reader too often.
>
> This comes down to personal preference, but (capitalizing words/using bold/underlining words/overusing italics, etc.) won't score any extra points from a reader. Overemphasizing too much is more likely to cause a distraction while reading, which can create a negative impression.

EXPOSITION IS CONFUSING

In early drafts, it's not uncommon to find scripts that still feel very much in the writer's head, meaning that although the writer may know their story inside out, not every necessary detail has been written down on the page. If vital information isn't being disclosed, or is being revealed at the wrong time or in the wrong order, it can make a story difficult to follow.

If there's a heated argument happening between a husband and wife in the kitchen, for example, but the mother-in-law suddenly interrupts half way through without the writer ever mentioning she was present when setting the scene at the beginning, then it's going to cause the reader to come out of the story to question logic.

The same applies to time period. If it's not mentioned that the story is taking place in the 1970s until page 10, for example, then the readers just spent ten pages imagining the story taking place in the present day. Adding a super, including the date in the scene heading, or having a recognizable visual that tells the reader exactly which era we're in would've avoided any unnecessary confusion here. Equally, if there are time jumps taking place, the writer needs to make it clear to both the reader and viewer that this is happening.

Similarly, with setting. Imagine how a few Christmas decorations mentioned in the description of the first few scenes would work much better to establish the story world than if it was left until much further to reveal that the story is set during the festive period.

Advise writers they need to get into the habit of telling us what we can see on screen *and* the order that we see it.

> **CHEATS**
>
> Make sure that everything in the script is as clear as possible to avoid creating any unwanted confusion for the reader.
>
> At times, exposition is creating confusion rather than informing, so make sure to tell us what we can see on screen and the order in which we see it. The reader needs to know (specific example from the script) when we first encounter this (character/action/setting, etc.) not (however many pages later it's delivered in the script) later, for example.
>
> Do more to clearly establish each scene more effectively. We need to know where we are, who is present, and what action is taking place on the screen *before* any dialogue is spoken. Think visuals first to avoid creating any confusion for the reader.

CHARACTER NAMES ARE INCONSISTENT

It's easy to tell when a writer has changed a character's name during a rewrite, as new and never mentioned before characters suddenly appear in the middle of a scene. Errors like this should hopefully get picked up via a thorough proofread by the writer, but if it happens frequently enough, causing you to pause and question logic, then it's worth making a general statement about double checking all character names are correct.

There's a tendency for writers to introduce characters by their entire full name, even though we'll only ever hear them be referred to by their first name. This is only something to mention if the writer desperately needs to cut back the word usage to help trim the page count, but why list ROBERT (BOBBY) HAMILTON-SMYTHE as a character when the audience will only ever know them as BOBBY. The same applies when a character's name is different to the one that the other characters actually use.

```
                MRS. HUNTER
        Here's your ticket, Alice.

                MISS THOMPSON
        Thanks, Sue.
```

Point out that inconsistent character names risk confusing the reader, which is something they need to avoid.

> **CHEATS**
>
> It's obvious that character names have changed at some stage during the rewrite as there are (several/some/a few, etc.) instances where an old name appears. Do a pass looking for any changes that may have been missed to avoid creating any confusion.
>
> If the audience are only ever going to know (character) by that name, then keep things simple by only using that name when delivering dialogue. Referring to them as (example from the script) risks confusing the reader, so avoid this by keeping things consistent.
>
> Cut anything that the audience doesn't need to know. If the viewers are only ever going to know (character) by that name, then don't include their entire full name and/or nickname in the scene description. Don't make the read take any longer than it needs to be by including pointless information.

THERE ARE 'UNFILMABLES'

An 'unfilmable' is anything that's written in the script that the audience can't see on screen. It's perfectly fine to use one or two along the way, especially when writing character introductions or essence statements, where it can help paint a more vivid picture in the reader's mind, such as "always feels uncomfortable in her own skin" or "could charm the back legs off a donkey", and it's also okay to mention when something is missing from a scene, such as "the gun is gone!" or "the room is now empty", so there's no need to be overly stringent about this, but if there are obvious instances where the writer is spending too much time detailing information that isn't going to be picked up by the audience, it's worth pointing this out.

Writers usually include 'unfilmables' when they're telling us a character's inner thoughts and feelings, such as "Joe is crushed, but determined not to show it.", "The way Helen looks at Jean makes her remember all the times she hurt her in the past.", or "Currently a secretary, Lisa dreams of breaking into screenwriting." While this may elicit a certain expression or physical reaction from the actor playing the role, advise the writer to use subtext to show the emotion or reaction they visually want to express instead.

Backstory is also often unnecessarily added into the scene description such as "James used to work in construction but lost his job due to the pandemic." or "Bob sits at his usual spot at the bar." Again, while it may be of some importance to the cast or crew, these details won't be picked up by the audience, plus there's a high chance that they're not even pivotal details we really need to know, anyway.

Character relationships are another example of filling the page with wasted words. "Seated at the dinner table is Ben's Aunt Kay, her husband Richard, and their two young boys, Howard and Hugh", which feels like a long way to say "Ben's extended family". And unless it's visually clear or mentioned in dialogue, things such as "adopted-daughter", "step-brother", or "ex-girlfriend" could also be missed by the audience, who might easily think that they're watching a character's "birth-daughter", "best friend" or "sister" instead.

Also watch for instances where writer's try to sneak parallel action into a scene by adding description of actions that are happening out of shot which the viewers can't see such as, "Unaware that Jane is sneaking out of her bedroom window, Geoff smokes a cigar by the fireplace." Explain to the writer that the audience isn't reading their screenplay, they're watching it, so details such as this won't be picked up. If the writer insists on keeping the sentiment, they need to show it visually.

If the writer has frequently used old-fashioned terms such as "we see", "we hear", or "we also" in their description, it's also worth reminding them that writing like this gives off an amateur vibe that they may want to avoid. Not only does wording like this pull the reader out of the story world to remind them they're reading a screenplay, they're almost always redundant words that are needlessly taking up precious space on the page. Remove the words and the writing still pulls focus onto the subject, "~~we see~~ a gun on the table", but uses fewer words, and is arguably making a more poignant statement.

> **CHEATS**
>
> Don't clutter up the page with 'unfilmables'. If we can't see something on screen, then generally, it doesn't need to be included in the script.
>
> Be mindful of including too many 'unfilmables' such as (provide specific examples from the script), which gives us information we can't see on screen, making it a potential cut.
>
> Keep in mind that the audience aren't reading the script, they're watching the movie, so information such as (give specific examples from the script) won't be picked up by the viewers. If we can't see it on screen, it very likely doesn't need to be mentioned at all.

THE SCRIPT NEEDS MORE POLISH

If you're writing coverage for an already competently written screenplay where there aren't any particularly major issues that need tackled, then focus on advising the writer on how to maximize the script's potential to sell. Pinpoint one or two areas that need tidying up that will give the script a more professional and polished look. This can be anything from mentioning small formatting mistakes, proofreading errors, or other inconsistencies in the writing.

Highlight anything that's giving off an amateur vibe, such as using "we hear", "close-up on Tom's face", or having too many CUT TO: transitions on the page. Would the script benefit from having a slightly longer or shorter page count? Are there any big chunks of text that slow the read? Would trimming out any ineffective redundant wording help create a tighter script, etc.?

> **CHEATS**
>
> Although the story is well-crafted and feels sufficiently developed, there are still some rookie errors that risk giving the script an unprofessional look, such as (list the primary errors needing to be fixed and how to correct them). The more polished the script is, the fewer reasons there are for a reader to turn it down.

> **CHEATS CONT.**
>
> There's always room for one more polish, no matter how well-crafted the story is, so ensure that (the formatting is flawless/wording is lean and evocative/orphans have been eliminated from the page, etc.) during the next rewrite.
>
> At this well-developed stage, it's all about polishing the script to ensure that it's 100% industry-ready and that there's absolutely no reason for a reader to turn this script down. There are a few easy-to-fix errors such as (examples from the script and how to correct them), that, once corrected, will help to give the script the polished professional look it needs.

SCENE DESCRIPTION

Scene direction can often be overlooked by the writer as simply being a list of instructions, and it's common to see amateur writers compose scene description as though they were giving stage directions instead. Ideally, the description is where writers should display their unique writing voice the most, engaging with the reader, and visually evoking each scene, but this isn't always the case with newbie writers.

Consider making a comment if;

WRITING IS NOVELISTIC

Novelistic writing contains a whole host of elements that aren't particularly well suited to screenwriting. Found most frequently in absolute beginner scripts, where the writer has naively thought that writing a screenplay is much the same as writing a novel, or in adaptations, where the writer has tried to mimic too much of the original material. Novelistic writing relies too much on telling, rather than showing, so there might be a lot of blatant exposition in the dialogue, a melodramatic tone to the action, over-description of the location, and a lot of 'unfilmables', which detail character's thoughts, backstory, and other irrelevant information that doesn't advance the story.

Novelistic writers may also be guilty of having a passive writing voice or using past tense, which forces the reader to do more work than they need to, making the read less engaging in the process. Advise readers to keep the visuals in mind when writing. We need to know what we can see on the screen and the order in which we see it. Usually, anything that can't be seen should be cut. Then the writer can focus on limiting the information and only detailing the actions, props, and dialogue that are pivotal for the story to move forward.

Further to this is sentence structure; placing the most important words first in order to keep things active. "The orange is eaten by Gail", for example, puts the emphasis on the orange, which is passive, as opposed to "Gail eats the orange" which makes the character active. How much detail you go into here depends on how novelistic the writing is, but it usually boils down to giving a reminder of the 'show, don't tell' mantra.

> **CHEATS**
>
> More work is needed to elevate the writing from being overly novelistic to more cinematic.
>
> Anything that we can't see on the screen, such as (list examples from the script) doesn't need to be in the script. Novelistic description like this is cluttering up the page, slowing the read, and can lead to a negative impression.
>
> At times, the script reads more like a novel than it does a screenplay. Cut back on the space-filling description, such as (examples from the script), the 'unfilmables', such as (examples from the script), and melodramatic action directions, such as (examples from the script), which will help get to the story much quicker, increase the pace, and make the script leaner.
>
> There's a fine line between evoking the scene in the reader's mind and going overboard with too much description. If something isn't advancing the plot, it doesn't need to be in the script, so avoid novelistic writing and try to focus only on the lines and actions that are actively pushing the story forward, rather than bogging it down with unnecessary detail.

GENRE ISN'T REFLECTED IN THE TONE

If you're reading a drama, the scene description in a script needs to be as emotionally engaging as the story that's unfolding on the page. If it's a horror, then the description better be making the hairs on the back of your neck stand up. A thriller needs to be nail-biting and in a comedy, the description needs to be as entertaining as the visual and vocal gags on the screen, etc.

If the tone of the writing isn't telling you what the genre is, especially during those pivotal first few pages, then the writer isn't doing themselves any favors. Sometimes it's just a case of reminding the writer that they can and should use scene description to evoke and emotionally engage just as much as the characters, the action, and the dialogue. Other times, you may need to point out that the tone that's coming across in the description is clashing with the genre of the story. If you've got a thriller plot but the tone of the writing is very sarcastic or comedic, then it's going to lessen the tension, drama, and suspense that should be coming across. Advising writers read other screenplays written in their chosen genre and to take note of how the writer uses description to evoke tone is recommended.

> **CHEATS**
>
> Don't be afraid to add tone to the scene description to help establish genre. Remember, a script needs to be just as (entertaining/gripping/engrossing, etc.) to read as it will be to watch, and writing compelling scene description will achieve this.
>
> The genre of this screenplay needs to be clear from the first few pages, so use more evocative scene description to add more (horror, humor, romance, etc.) to help show this.
>
> Keeping in mind that this is a (horror, fantasy, drama, etc.), at times the tone of the writing clashes with that. (provide a specific example from the script that highlights this issue and an explanation about why this is a problem). Do a tonal pass to ensure that the emotion trying to be evoked in the audience during every scene is being reflected in the word choice too.

ORPHANS NEED TO BE CUT

This note is probably more useful for short or TV scripts, but if the page count is a little on the high side, the script looks untidy, or the writer just needs to be leaner in their delivery, advise doing a pass that eliminates orphans - the one or two words that take up an entire line on the page to themselves in either the scene description or the dialogue. This isn't exactly an essential rewrite pass to do, and it's unlikely that a script would ever be rejected for this reason, but it will force a writer to examine their word choice more thoroughly and help them find ways of saying the same thing, but with fewer, more effective words.

CHEATS
The script is already at a well-developed stage, meaning that the script really only needs further polish. Eliminating 'orphans' on the page is will help to give the script a much leaner and tighter look.
One way to help trim down the page count is to eliminate any 'orphans' on the page. Orphans are the one or two words at the end of a sentence that takes up a whole line to themselves on the page.
Consider rewording sentences to cut back on the amount of 'orphans' on the page. Not only will this shave a little off the page count, it'll make sentences leaner and more effective too.

SENTENCE STRUCTURE IS POOR

This can occur at any stage of script development, and isn't always something that the writer only needs to focus on during a final polish. Badly written scene description can stagger the flow of the read, forcing the reader to stop and re-read lines. Delivering information in the wrong order can cause the plot to be unnecessarily confusing. Not mixing up sentence length can lead to a monotonous read, and using the same words repeatedly makes the writer look sloppy.

Again, solving this issue goes back to recommending that the writer reads other scripts and practicing the craft. Advise readers to go through each sentence with a fine-tooth comb if necessary. How many words can they strip out of a sentence without it losing its meaning? Ask them to do a pass looking specifically for words or phrases that are being used too frequently and to try and mix things up a little. The writer needs to make sure that the information being delivered on the page is in the same order that the audience will see it appear on screen. If punctuation is the root cause of poor sentence structure, suggest the writer has the script thoroughly proofread before submitting it elsewhere.

CHEATS

Poor spelling and grammar is having a detrimental effect on the read, with enough errors occurring to keep interrupting the flow, distract the reader's eyes, and create unnecessary confusion. A thorough proofread is advised.

Screenwriting is about telling a story in as few words as possible, so always be on the lookout for ways to say the same thing, but with fewer words. Take (examples from the script) for example, which could easily be re-worded as (reader's suggestion) without losing any effect. Other tactics involve not stating the obvious, not unnecessarily repeating words or information, and limiting decorative scene descriptions. All of which will help create a leaner, more powerful screenplay.

A harsh edit focusing on sentence structure is needed to make the script as engaging to read as it will be to watch. Reading the entire script out loud is highly recommended here. Not only will this help find clunky sentences, repetitive wording, and over-written description, it'll help proofread the script at the same time too.

DIALOGUE IS WRITTEN IN THE SCENE DESCRIPTION

This is a variation of the writer telling us information we already know, or more importantly, what we're about to discover.

```
INT. CAFÉ - DAY

At a booth, Paul and Tony are discussing the meeting
they've just had back at the office.
                    PAUL
          Wow, is the new manager a douche,
          or what?
```
Remind the writer that the audience aren't reading the screenplay, they're watching the story unfold on screen, so detailing info that's about to happen

is wasting space on the page. Note that in the above example, there's no sense of evocative scene setting occurring. The description isn't suggestive of the tone or atmosphere, there's a lack of visual detail, and there's no action or movement either. While none of those things are absolute must-haves when setting a scene, they're great at engaging with the reader and pulling them into the story.

> **CHEATS**
>
> Don't waste space on the page telling us what's about to happen. Tell us what *is* happening instead. Take (use an example from the script) for example. The lines of dialogue from (character) tell us all the information we need to know, rendering ("quote the damaging scene description") pointless.
>
> Try not to waste space on the page by repeating information unnecessarily. If (character) says ("quote a line from the script"), then you don't need to tell us ("quote the scene description that preceded the dialogue") beforehand. Consider using the page space to set the scene more effectively by revealing tone, adding action, or inserting visuals instead.

THERE'S TOO MUCH SCENE DESCRIPTION

Getting the balance between not having enough description and having too much can be difficult. Some genres will need more time spent on world-building, detailing busy action sequences, or describing period settings etc., but it's easy to spot when writers are perhaps going overboard with the detail. Text-heavy pages are a big give away, whether that's description, dialogue, or both. A reader will immediately know that the script is going to take longer than usual to get through, which isn't the best first impression to make. There's also the risk that a reader may skim read to speed up the process and miss pivotal info, all of which can be pointed out to the writer if needed.

If the scene heading tells us we're in an office, for example, the reader's going to naturally assume that there are chairs, desks, filing cabinets, and photocopier etc. Encourage the writer to write economically by saying the same thing but with fewer words as much as possible. `"Maria grabs the oven glove, removes the Moroccan lamb stew from the oven and places it as the centerpiece of the table."` is not only boring to read, it's also a really long way to simply say "Maria serves dinner".

Remind the writer that we don't need to know absolutely everything. Unless something is absolutely pivotal to the plot, we probably don't need to know the color of someone's eyes, the flavor of the soup they're drinking, or every single piece of furniture that's in a room. Less is more. Usually, all that needs to be described is the visual action that's happening on screen, not the surrounding decoration.

CHEATS
Screenwriting is all about telling a powerful story in as few words as possible, so be careful not to go overboard when writing scene description.
Using a few choice visuals to help establish a scene is much more powerful and efficient than writing boring lists of every item in a location. (provide an example of a shortened version of the over-description in the script to help highlight this, such as "typical gamers bedroom" or "dive bar", etc.)
Be careful not to clutter up the page by going into too much detail in the scene description. Is it really necessary that we know (example from the script), that (character) is wearing (example from the script), or that (overly specific detail from the script)? If something isn't pivotal to the story, it doesn't need to be included. Too much description can slow the read and hamper the pace of the story, so execute a harsh edit to minimize the decoration.

SCENE DESCRIPTION REPEATS INFORMATION

The writer is only wasting precious story-telling space on the page when they use scene description to tell us something that we already know. This isn't referring to when a writer is repeating a piece of pivotal information as a plot point reminder, but rather when they're pointing out the obvious or repeating info without purpose.

Some examples include when rookie writers don't understand that EXT. is short for external, such as:

```
EXT. IN FRONT OF BEN'S HOME
or
EXT. OUTSIDE THE VAN
```

When the scene heading is repeated in the description:

```
EXT. CHRYSLER BUILDING - DAY

Darlene and Jason converge at the glass doors of the
Chrysler Building.
```

It also includes when writers waste time by stating the obvious:

"He picks the glass up with his hand" – what else would he be picking it up with?
or
"Light shines through the glass window" – what windows aren't made from glass?

Or when the writer tells us something that we've just watched happen on screen or is about to happen, as opposed to describing the action *as it happens*.

```
Louise shouts a warning.

                    LOUISE
          He's coming!
```

If there's space to point out specific instances in your report, do so, because if writers are doing this, they probably aren't aware, but need to be.

CHEATS

Try not to waste space on the page by telling us something we already know, such as (use examples from the script), which slows the pace of both the read and the story.

When polishing the script, look to remove any instances of stating the obvious, such as (use an example from the script), or are repeating information we already know, such as (use an example from the script). This will help trim off the fat and make the script much leaner.

VITAL INFO IS MISSING OR IN THE WRONG ORDER

If a reader needs to stop in order to re-read a line or question logic, it's breaking the immersion into the story world, which a writer needs to avoid as much as possible. There's no easy way to tell a writer that their description is confusing, but it needs to be said. Again, find examples in the script that you can use to highlight the problem. Sugar-coat the note by saying that the writer's enthusiasm during the scene is very evident, but that they need to take a step back to make sure that everyone who reads their script is privy to all the information that they need. Possibly point out that the story feels still very much in the writer's head instead of being down on the page, which means while they may know all the necessary info, the reader doesn't.

In cases where info isn't being delivered in the correct order, such as starting a new scene with a line of dialogue instead of establishing the setting, remind the writer that they need to keep the visuals at the forefront of their mind when writing. We need to know what we can see on screen before audio is mentioned, and we also need to be told the order in which we can see and hear everything, otherwise the writer risks confusing the reader.

CHEATS

At this stage, the story feels like it's still very much in the writer's head, rather than down on the page, which means there are a few (missing pieces of info/instances of exposition being delivered in the wrong order) that can easily confuse someone who's reading the script for the first time.

Do a pass to make sure that everything is as clear on the page as it can be. It's hard to imagine reading a script for the very first time with no prior knowledge of the story or characters, but that's the mindset needed when tackling rewrites. At present, there's a lot of pivotal info not being given and that creates plot holes, which might stop a reader from enjoying the story.

Some confusion is being caused by (missing info/or info being delivered in the wrong order), such as (specific examples from the script), so make sure to (fill in any potential plot holes/tell us what we can see on screen in the order that we see it).

ACTORS ARE BEING OVER DIRECTED

Detailing every single movement that a character makes can hamper the pace of a scene, but ultimately, it isn't very interesting to read. Similarly, actors rarely want to be instructed on every single movement they should take either. They want to bring their own interpretation to the part, not to have their creativity crippled by having to follow a strict set of instructions.

An easy way to spot a new writer is that they seem to think that everyone grins. "(grinning wildly)", "they all grin back", or "wearing a boyish grin". It's a novelistic term, and it's unimaginative too. "she turns her head towards the sound", "punches the wall with his left fist", or even something more subtle such as "bites her bottom lip" can all be viewed as over directing. You shouldn't be highlighting every instance that a writer directs the actor here. If an instruction adds something to the story, helps evoke the mood, and enhances the read, then yes, by all means keep them in the script, but if there are too many directions giving unnecessary specifics that clutter up the page and hamper the pace, then yes, absolutely make a comment.

Point out to the writer exactly why over directing the actors is having a detrimental effect on their script and ask them to consider revealing more about what emotions and feelings a character is experiencing rather than detailing any actions that they think are expressing those emotions. This almost goes against the 'show, don't tell' mantra here, but think of it as creating visual subtext instead.

CHEATS

Be careful not to over direct the actors by detailing every single action that they take, such as (examples from the script). These will more than likely be dismissed by the actors as they'll want to bring their own interpretation of the character to the screen.

Rather than indicate every single movement a character takes, such as (examples from the script), consider expressing the emotion, mood, or tone behind the action and allow the actors to interpret this instead.

> **CHEATS CONT.**
>
> Although directing the actors every action, such as (examples from the script) has the sense of writing visually, as it's showing, not telling, unfortunately, it's not terribly engaging to read. It's worth avoiding over-directing the action and focusing on conveying the emotion of the characters instead. This allows the actor to put their own stamp on the character and it's more compelling for the reader at the same time too.

THERE'S TOO MUCH DETAIL

This can be quite common in stories that need a lot of world building, such as alien worlds, fantasy settings, period pieces, or futuristic locations, but it's equally just as common to see this be done by new writers who feel the need to physically describe absolutely everything we can see on the screen. Unless it's essential that we know that `"the fireplace is to the right of the door"`, that `"the antique couch is covered in soft brown leather"` or that `"a large flat screen TV hangs on the wall in the bar"`, (and trust me, it never is), then over embellished details such as this are pointlessly taking up precious space on the page.

The same applies to character clothing, the way the lights shines through a window, and what individual extras are doing in the background. Yes, the writer can use description to convey tone and evoke mood, but basically anything that isn't advancing the plot should be considered as a potential cut.

Remind the writer that it's the job of the wardrobe department, the set designers, and the cinematographers etc. to come up with the fine details that decorate a production and that by inserting too much description in their script, while they may think that the visuals are helping to paint a clearer picture in the readers mind, if they're unimportant pieces of information, they're essentially hampering the pace of the story and getting in the way of the more interesting characters, action, and dialogue that's happening on the page instead. Again, less is more, and a few carefully selected words can be much more engaging to read.

> **CHEATS**
>
> Don't feel the need to list every object and prop in the room when starting a scene in a new location. It's not exactly entertaining to read and it risks cluttering up the page with unnecessary details. We all know what a (example location from the script) looks like, so consider evoking the mood, atmosphere, or tone of the scene instead of painting too many fine details.
>
> Try not to bog the story down by over-describing the visuals. Unless a prop, object, item of clothing, etc. is pivotal to the plot, it probably doesn't need to be in the script, so concentrate on setting the scene by evoking the mood or atmosphere instead.
>
> There's a fine line between painting a specific picture in the reader's mind and hampering the pace of the story by filling the page with details that aren't particularly pivotal. Take (instance from the script) for example, where telling us that (unnecessary details) isn't adding anything to the story, meaning it won't harm the script if it's removed either.

OVER DIRECTING

There's a fine line between a writer trying to show that they can write with the visuals in mind, and them hoping to show that they can direct the screenplay themselves. It's understandable that a writer wants to relay their vision as clearly as possible, but this often leads to them trying to do everyone else's job for them, so it's important to remind the writer to stick to what they do best; telling the story.

Reading already produced scripts, aka shooting scripts, can also give a false impression on how to format a screenplay for those none the wiser, so it could be a case of a writer picking up the wrong information when researching.

A well-written script should immerse the reader into the story as much as possible and all camera directions, transitions, and cumbersome scene headings do is to remind the reader that they're reading a screenplay, which ironically, is something a writer should avoid.

Consider making a comment if;

THERE ARE TOO MANY CAMERA DIRECTIONS

It's understandable that a newbie writer wants to get behind the camera and direct each and every shot on the page just as they imagine it, but the reality is that these are ultimately decisions that the director will want to make themselves. When spec scripts sell, it's extremely rare that the studio will allow a new writer to also direct, unless they have a solid body of produced work behind them to prove that they're capable.

Camera directions in both feature and TV pilot scripts are often a big giveaway that the writer is amateur, as an experienced writer should know how to direct the camera in much subtler ways, and this is what you should encourage too. In short scripts, however, there's every possibility that the writer is also planning on directing, so keep this in mind when making comments.

"We ZOOM IN on Joe's face" or "ANGLE ON Joe" both imply the writer wants us to focus on a specific character, but it isn't telling us what emotions the character is feeling or how they're reacting to whatever's happening. Something like "Joe is stunned" not only conveys the emotion of the scene, it also highly implies the need for a close-up shot there too. Simply cutting the camera direction is usually effective enough. "~~CLOSE-UP on~~ the empty suitcase". "~~ZOOM IN on~~ the blood-stained carpet". Take away the direction and the writing still indicates where the camera should be focusing, plus it uses fewer words.

Discourage writers from using any camera direction, especially completely unnecessary ones, such as aerial shots, dolly shots, wide shots, or zooms. Remind them they shouldn't be taking on the role of editor, director, or cinematographer, and should stick to the job of writing the story effectively and efficiently.

CHEATS

Inserting camera directions aren't recommended in a spec script as it's highly unlikely that a new writer will be also be given the task of directing the script too. Add to that, camera directions are just another reminder that the reader is reading a screenplay when ideally, they should be immersed into the story world as much as possible, so they're well-worth removing.

> **CHEATS CONT.**
>
> While camera directions are great at indicating that a writer is thinking visually, they're not something that should be included in a spec script. Remove them and save them for the shooting script if the piece sells.
>
> If the writing is strong enough, specific camera directions can be implied without being so literal. Drawing attention to an action, character, prop, etc., in the scene direction can often be enough to suggest a close-up, for example (use an example from the script to show the effectiveness of cutting a camera direction or rewording a sentence to highlight this)
>
> Unless the writer is also planning on directing the script too, all camera directions can be cut. If the script sells, these will likely be removed regardless, so they're essentially just taking up precious space on the page.

THERE ARE UNNECESSARY SHOT TRANSITIONS

Scene transitions are necessary direction in a shooting script, but unless a transition is pivotal to the plot, pace, or style, they're not something that's going to be needed in a spec script. The only transitions that are required are `FADE IN:` and `FADE OUT:` but even omitting these is now acceptable in a modern script.

`CUT TO:` is being used less and less in scripts too as it's deemed to just take up too much room on the page, plus it pulls the reader out of the story world to remind them they're reading a screenplay (again!). Other transitions such as `DISSOLVE TO:`, `SMASH CUT:`, `JUMP CUT:`, and `MATCH CUT:` are very likely going to be completely ignored by the director or cut if the script does finally go into production, so why waste vital story-telling space on the page to use them?

Advise writers to minimize the use of transitions as much as possible, as they're distracting on the page and they're not really adding anything to the story.

> **CHEATS**
>
> Like camera directions, shot transitions should rarely be used in a spec script and they should only be used when they're crucial to the story. (use an example of misusing a transition from the script to highlight this)
>
> Shot transitions such as (take instances that have been used in the script) are editing choices for the editor or director to make, rather than the screenwriter. In the instances that they've been used here, they're not particularly adding anything to the plot, so consider removing these distractions on the page, which will also help free up some vital story-telling space.
>
> Try not to overuse shot transitions throughout the script. Not only do they take up a lot of page space, they also risk distracting the reader's eye during the read.

VISUALS

Surprisingly, new writers can very quickly forget that film is a visual medium and over rely on dialogue to tell the story instead. Visual storytelling is all about using imagery to convey complex thoughts and emotions without using too much dialogue, but writing visually can be incredibly difficult. It's easier to have a character deliver information via dialogue, so it's understandable why so many writers struggle with this aspect of storytelling, but having too much on-the-nose speech like this not only lessens the realism, it slows the pace of the story too, as it takes longer to convey information via dialogue than it does with a visual.

Consider making a comment if;

THE WRITER IS TELLING, NOT SHOWING

It's easy to get carried away during a big important monologue or when two characters are bouncing off one another in a fast-paced conversation, and audiences love these moments just as much too, but when a reader comes across pages of nothing but dialogue, not only is it safe to assume that half of it can probably be cut without harming the overall meaning, there's usually a clear sign the writer has forgotten about the visuals during those scenes too.

Remind the writer that film is primarily a visual medium and while yes, dialogue absolutely plays a pivotal part in storytelling, the viewers will essentially pay more attention to what they can see as opposed to what they can hear. It's called a movie for a reason; there are images moving on the screen, but scenes laden with dialogue could be interpreted as static, uninteresting, and tedious, and that risks the viewers tuning out while listening because there's probably not a lot happening on screen to keep their eyes busy.

Encourage the writer to break up long pieces of dialogue with a visual. This can be anything from a reaction shot of another character, characters taking action while talking, or having something happening in the background. Anything that creates movement can help keep the viewers engaged, plus it's another way to add another layer to the story.

As already mentioned, of course, it's easier to tell a story using dialogue than with visuals. We're used to hearing stories be told to us verbally in our daily lives and storytelling in novels is mostly communicated to us from a narrator's point of view, so we're all extremely used to being told, rather than shown information.

'Show, don't tell' should be a familiar term to you, but many aspiring writers can become confused about what this actually means. If a piece of information can be delivered by using a visual instead of a line of dialogue, it can often lead to a more powerful and memorable message being conveyed. It's the longing glance that the hero gives his secret love that tells us how much he's into her, as opposed to us hearing him confessing his love to her to his best friend instead. It's when we see how bad-ass the villain is rather than listen to the hero talk about how bad-ass they are. And it's the protagonist Facebook stalking their ex instead of simply saying "I miss you".

You'll be able to recognize when writers are delivering too much exposition via dialogue as not only will the script feel overly talky, often characters will talk in a very on-the-nose manner at the same time too. People rarely blurt out whatever they're thinking or feeling in real life (refer to the DIALOGUE IS TOO ON-THE-NOSE chapter for more information on how to combat this particular issue) and while yes, there are certainly instances where this type of talk can work effectively in a scene, if it's happening all the time, it's probably because the writer forgot to use visuals to tell the story.

This is a common issue to find in early drafts, so don't be too harsh, but it's worth asking the writer to examine whether any of the exposition being delivered in the dialogue could be given visually instead. Would a character's silence speak more volumes? Could it be more effective to indicate the character's emotions in the scene description and let the actor interpret that rather than have them spell it out verbally? What's going to be more interesting for the audience? Hearing about it, or watching it?

CHEATS

Be careful not to tell the story primarily using dialogue instead of showing the story through action. Film is a visual medium, so the viewers are going to be paying a lot more attention to what they can see on screen as opposed to what they can hear. More showing and less telling is advised here, so look for any exposition-heavy dialogue that could be delivered visually instead.

This is a fairly talky piece, and while there are some wonderful pieces of dialogue in there, don't forget 'show, don't tell'. Take (example from the script) for instance. What's going to be more interesting for the viewers here? Listening to (exposition) or watching (exposition)? If information can be delivered visually or through action, it can often deliver a more powerful and memorable punch.

At times, it almost feels as though the visuals have been forgotten about, with lots of long-winded dialogue with minimal action happening on screen. Consider adding more movement to stagnant scenes, whether that's by inserting a quick cutaway shot of a reaction or by having characters undertake an action while delivering dialogue. It's important to keep the audience's eyes busy just as much as their ears.

THE CONCLUSION

Here's where you sum up all the major points in your report highlighting the essential areas that a writer should work on first. Don't simply regurgitate everything you've already talked about. It's not uncommon for a reader to have some fresh insights when collecting their thoughts at the end of a report, and adding in some extra comments helps to bring more value to this section too. Using brief bullet-point statements can work effectively here, especially if you're trying to adhere to a page limit or focus on the one or two big issues that's currently holding the script back.

Always start off with, you've guessed it, a positive note. Even if every category technically "needs work", there are usually some areas that the writer had a more solid grip on than others, so feel free to highlight those areas to the writer too.

> *"There's a great foundation on which to build here."*
> *"There's lots to love about this script."*
> *"There's plenty of potential in both the premise and the writing."*

No matter how much of a slog reading the script and writing the report has been, remember "your report is supposed to help and encourage the writer, not criticize them to the point that they'll never want to write a screenplay ever again", so ensure that your concluding comments are geared up to make the writer excited about the rewriting process by highlighting the positive results that will come from implementing your recommended changes.

It can be very difficult to take criticism, no matter how helpful it is, so depending on how formal you're allowed to be, ending on a positive word of encouragement or upbeat piece of praise can help boost a writer's confidence. A "well done" or "great effort" can go a long way to ensure that the writer feels like they're on the right path. Everyone's got to start somewhere and no one does it brilliantly the first time, but with your help, a writer's next draft or next script can be, which means a job well done for you too.

CHEATS

Overall, these comments are mostly small nit-picks due to the script already being in excellent condition. Use them to prepare for future notes from producers and execs where you can either be equipped to make the suggested changes or to be able to justify why changes shouldn't be made.

The great concept sells this piece alone and at this stage, there's very little needing addressed. Concentrate on polishing the script in order to ensure that it's industry-ready.

There's a strong genre piece here that has the potential to do extremely well.

The writer shows experience, confidence, and competency in their writing.

This is a (fun/farcical/fresh/fascinating, etc.) story that's well written and has lots to offer. With a great deal to like, there's a solid foundation on which to build.

VERDICT

Whether you're assessing a screenplay for a studio, writing coverage for a client, or judging a contest entry, it's not uncommon for the script to be rated as a Pass, Consider, or Recommend.

PASS is the most frequently given verdict, so don't feel too guilty about using it. A reader will often be able to gauge this outcome as early as the first page of a screenplay. Incorrect formatting, text-heavy pages, and poor dialogue are instant indicators of a screenwriter's ability. Passing on a script doesn't mean that it should be swiftly dragged to the desktop trashcan. It simply means that the piece needs significant work to make it a viable project.

CONSIDER should indicate that a script has commercial potential, but that it also still requires some minor adjustments (aka further rewrites). It's a positive rating that can help move a script closer up the ladder if the right adjustments are made. It means that a script is close to being production-ready and that there's also something compelling about it.

RECOMMEND should be used with caution, and only awarded to scripts that are industry-ready, highly polished, and close to being green-lit. For contest readers, this is you stating that you've read the winning script and for studio readers, this is you saying to your boss that if you reject this great script, you'll both be fired.

WHAT NOW?

If you're completely new to script reading, practice is what's going to help you the most. Offer to write coverage for your peers to get some much-needed experience. There's no shortage of writers out there desperately looking for someone to read their script, so go to your writing friends, your immediate network, or further afield.

Back when I was just starting out, I wrote peer reviews on the now extinct Trigger Street Labs website which operated on a points system. If you wanted other writers to read and review your script, you had to read and review at least 5 or 10 other scripts first. That was where I quickly learned that not all feedback was equal. Some writers would just leave an unhelpful account of what they did or didn't like, while others gave great comprehensive breakdowns and useful pointers. It's also where I learned that not every writer can take constructive criticism. "But you obviously don't understand…", yes, because it wasn't clear in your script! It was a great training ground that also got new eyes on my own projects too.

Here's a short list of where you can begin to find screenplays to read, write coverage on, and gain some experience:

ScriptMother is a similar platform to Trigger Street Labs that's worth investigating. It's "an online screenwriting network for members to engage with a community of fellow writers and receive valuable reviews for their work. Writers earn "script points" for reviewing work by fellow scriptwriters that can be used to submit their own scripts for reviews."

Talentville also offers writers the ability to "upload screenplays you have written to our online library, get feedback and reviews from other Residents and ultimately see how your work is received. In return you will be asked to read the work of other writers and write reviews that they can use to improve the quality of their writing."

CoverflyX is a "a free service that allows writers to get peer notes on their screenplays in return for Coverfly tokens. Coverfly tokens have no monetary value and cannot be sold or bought. Instead, writers can earn tokens by providing notes on the work of other Coverfly users, and in turn they can exchange those tokens for feedback on their own projects."

r/Screenwriting and **r/ReadMyScript** are both great subreddits to find aspiring screenwriters actively seeking feedback on their scripts, and for anyone looking to just start reading screenplays, you can't beat **simplyscripts.com**, which has a database of hundreds of downloadable film and TV screenplays as well as unproduced spec scripts on there too.

WHERE TO FIND SCRIPT READER JOBS

There are many companies, organizations, and individuals within the film and TV industry that require script readers.

For those just starting out, be prepared to work pro-bono until you find your feet and have gained enough experience to warrant payment, but if you already have sufficient education or experience and can demonstrate you understand what's required, you should be able to go straight into a paid position.

Prepare your resume, have coverage samples ready to prove your abilities, and start hunting. Here's a list of who might require hired readers:

- Screenplay contests
- Coverage services
- Literary agents
- Studios
- Broadcasters
- Film festivals
- Training organizations
- Funding schemes or bodies
- Production companies
- Independent producers
- Film distributers
- Film financiers
- Film sales agents
- Talent agents
- Actors themselves
- Theatres

For further info on all things script reading, including which screenplay contests to apply to and when to find script reading work, visit my official website here: **www.scriptreaderscheatsheet.com**

INDEX

A
accents, 147, 148
Act I, 69-72, 76, 77
Act II, 78
Act III, 89-90,
act breaks, 54, 68, 77-78
adaptation, 47, 48, 52, 56, 175
antagonist, 88, 90, 96, 111, 124-128, 129
autobiography, 46

B
backstory, 105-106, 125-126, 137, 173, 175
beat sheet, 46, 52, 76, 78
believability, 43, 46, 60, 61-64, 74, 106, 122, 149
Blank Coverage Template, 23
budget, 52, 55, 59, 64-68, 129

C
camera directions, 187
casting, 26, 50, 60, 65, 96-98, 117,
cast size, 87, 132
character, 96-136
character arc, 37, 76, 79, 107, 109, 116, 121-124,
character archetypes, 34, 116, 132
character goals, 81, 83, 103-106, 111, 134, 135,
character introductions, 70, 93, 96-102, 119, 130-132, 171-172
characterization, 96-136
Cheat Sheet Checklist, 17, 18
cliches, 34, 35, 44, 117, 132
conclusion, the, 192
conflict, 46, 70, 83-84, 111, 152
contest readers, 11
copyrighted material, 44, 45, 67
coverage readers, 12

D
dialogue, 137-150
diversity, 45, 60, 116-118, 133,
dramatic momentum, 43, 47-48, 65, 77, 113, 151-156

E
ensemble, 38, 87, 118, 121, 130-131
exposition, 137-146, 170-171

F
filler dialogue, 140-141, 143
flashbacks, 91-92,
flaws, weaknesses, and limitations, 106-110, 114, 120-121, 125,
formatting, 53-54, 157, 160-170

G
genre, 33-36, 47-48, 58, 176-177,
grade, 25

H
hooks, 69-70, 77, 78, 79-80, 152

I
inciting incident, 28, 71-72, 76-77

L
layout, 23-26
length, 49, 52-55
logline, 24, 27-28, 30

M
marketability, 55-61
medium, 49-51
midpoint, 77-79, 152

M
montage, 66, 90, 92-93
motivation, 61-63, 105, 122, 128

N
narrative devices, 90-95
novelistic description, 139, 175-176, 184

O
on-the-nose dialogue, 120, 139-140, 189-191
opening sequences, 41, 69-72, 76-77
originality, 44-49
over directing the actors, 164, 184-185, camera directions, 187 shot transitions, 188,

P
pace, 48, 81-85, 140-145, 151-156
parentheticals, 163-165
passive characters, 103, 133-136
plot holes, 63-64, 74, 183
premise, 30-68
protagonist, the, 46, 71, 83, 96, 103-110, 114-124, 134-136

Q
Q&A dialogue, 141-142

R
readability, 157-191
repetition, 82-83, 143, 144-145, 154-155
root-ability, 96, 114-120
rule of three, 94-95

S
scene headings, 42, 163, 168,
scene structure, 80-85
script reader jobs, 196

second act see Act II
secondary characters (supporting characters), 71, 86, 117-119, 128-133, 134
setups & payoffs, 39, 51, 72-75, 89, 97
stakes, 78, 104, 105, 110-114
story beats, 69, 76-80, 121
structure, 68-95
studio readers, 13-14
sub-plots, 39, 55, 86-90
subtext, 139-140,
supporting characters see secondary characters
synopsis, 21, 24, 29

T
theme, 36-40,
third act see Act III
title, 31-32
title page, 157-160
tone, 40-44
turning points see story beats
TV, 30, 38, 54, 71, 86,

U
unfilmables, 172-176

V
verdict, 194
visuals, 138, 145, 159, 175, 181, 185, 189-191

W
writing coverage, 19-29

THE CHEAT SHEET CHECKLIST

PREMISE

TITLE:
- [ ] The title is misleading
- [ ] The title could cause offence

THEME:
- [ ] The overall theme is unclear
- [ ] There are too many themes
- [ ] Subplots don't reflect theme
- [ ] Theme doesn't get resolved

ORIGINALITY:
- [ ] It's too similar to other stuff
- [ ] It's so unusual, it's confusing
- [ ] It's a boring true-life story
- [ ] It's a boring adaptation

LENGTH:
- [ ] It's too long or too short
- [ ] The page count is unrealistic
- [ ] Altering the page count will add desirability

BELIEVABILITY:
- [ ] Character actions are absurd
- [ ] There's noticeable plot holes

GENRE:
- [ ] Genre is unclear
- [ ] Doesn't add anything new
- [ ] Not enough conventions

TONE:
- [ ] Tone isn't immediately clear
- [ ] Tone isn't strong enough
- [ ] Tone is inconsistent

MEDIUM:
- [ ] It doesn't fit the format
- [ ] It doesn't have legs

MARKETABILITY:
- [ ] It only has niche appeal
- [ ] It won't please its audience
- [ ] It's trying to please everyone
- [ ] It lacks international appeal
- [ ] There's a lack of diversity

BUDGET:
- [ ] There's too many characters
- [ ] There's too many locations
- [ ] It uses copyrighted material

STRUCTURE

OPENING SEQUENCES:
- [ ] There's no hook
- [ ] The MC isn't in the first scene
- [ ] There's too much setup

STORY BEATS:
- [ ] The premise is unclear
- [ ] Turning points aren't clear
- [ ] There's a weak mid-point
- [ ] The end hook is weak

SETUPS & PAYOFFS:
- [ ] Setups aren't paid off
- [ ] Payoffs aren't setup
- [ ] Setups are too obvious

SCENE STRUCTURE:
- [ ] The plot doesn't advance
- [ ] Scenes repeat needless info
- [ ] Scenes have no conflict
- [ ] Scenes are too long

SUBPLOTS:
- [ ] There's a lack of subplots
- [ ] There are too many subplots
- [ ] Subplots don't connect to the A-story
- [ ] Subplots don't merge during the final act

NARRATIVE DEVICES:
- [ ] Flashbacks are unnecessary
- [ ] Montages are unnecessary
- [ ] Info is revealed in the wrong order
- [ ] The writer hasn't used the 'rule of three'

CHARACTER

CHARACTER INTRODUCTIONS:
- [ ] Physical appearances are too detailed
- [ ] Vital information is missing
- [ ] Action isn't revealing character
- [ ] Gender isn't immediately clear
- [ ] Character names are confusing
- [ ] Major characters aren't named
- [ ] Characters are numbered

STAKES:
- [ ] There are no clear stakes
- [ ] The stakes aren't big enough
- [ ] The stakes don't increase

CHARACTER ARC:
- [ ] The MC doesn't change
- [ ] Character arcs aren't believable
- [ ] The MC doesn't have actor bait

ANTAGONISTIC FORCE:
- [ ] There is no antagonistic character
- [ ] The antagonist isn't developed
- [ ] The antagonist lacks screen time
- [ ] The antagonist is a weak rival

GOALS:
- [ ] The MC has no clear goal
- [ ] The MC's goal is boring
- [ ] Motivations are unclear

FLAWS, WEAKNESSES, LIMITATIONS:
- [ ] The MC is too perfect
- [ ] The major flaw isn't tied to the central plot
- [ ] The MC's flaw doesn't become a strength

ROOT-ABILITY:
- [ ] The MC is too unlikable
- [ ] Characters are one-dimensional
- [ ] The cast lacks diversity
- [ ] It's unclear whose story it is
- [ ] Characters aren't engaging

SUPPORTING CHARACTERS:
- [ ] Minor characters overshadow
- [ ] Minor characters feature more
- [ ] Minor characters lack purpose
- [ ] Minor characters are flat

PASSIVE CHARACTERS:
- [ ] The MC isn't solving problems
- [ ] The MC doesn't drive change

DIALOGUE

EXPOSITION:
- [ ] There's too much dialogue
- [ ] Dialogue is too on-the-nose
- [ ] There's too much filler dialogue
- [ ] There's too much Q&A dialogue
- [ ] Dialogue repeats info
- [ ] Wording is repetitive
- [ ] There's too much technical talk

VOICE:
- [ ] Characters sound too alike
- [ ] Dialects are overused
- [ ] Dialogue isn't realistic

PACE

DRAMATIC MOMENTUM:
- [ ] There are lulls in the story
- [ ] There's no 'catch your breath' moments
- [ ] Repetition hampers the pace
- [ ] There's a lack of white space on the page

READABILITY

TITLE PAGE:
- [ ] There is no title page
- [ ] Contact details are missing
- [ ] The title page has unnecessary elements

PARENTHETICALS:
- [ ] Parentheticals are uncalled for
- [ ] Parentheticals are used too often

SCENE DESCRIPTION:
- [ ] Writing is novelistic
- [ ] Genre isn't reflected in the tone
- [ ] Orphans need to be cut
- [ ] Sentence structure is poor
- [ ] Dialogue is written in description
- [ ] There's too much description
- [ ] Vital info is missing
- [ ] Scene description repeats info
- [ ] Actors are being over directed
- [ ] There's too much detail

FORMATTING:
- [ ] The industry layout is incorrect
- [ ] There are too many formatting errors
- [ ] Scene headings are confusing

PRESENTATION:
- [ ] There are big paragraphs of text
- [ ] The script hasn't been proofread
- [ ] Scene headings are too long
- [ ] Bold or caps have been overused
- [ ] Exposition is confusing
- [ ] Names are inconsistent
- [ ] There are 'unfilmables'
- [ ] The script needs more polish

OVER DIRECTING:
- [ ] There's camera directions
- [ ] There are shot transitions

VISUALS:
- [ ] The writer is telling, not showing

Phew!

Glad that's over. If you got this far too, thank you for sticking with me! If you've any comments, queries, or questions, drop me a line at **scriptreaderscheatsheet@gmail.com** and if you're feeling especially generous, please consider leaving a review on whichever site you found this book. Positive reviews are what really helps push a book above the thousands of others out there, so that would be a massive help that would be greatly appreciated.

For more things script reading (and writing!) visit the website: **https://www.scriptreaderscheatsheet.com/** and feel free to sign up to the Script Reader newsletter for news, updates, and the occasional helpful workbook or two.

All the best to you in your screenwriting and script reading journey!

Made in the USA
Las Vegas, NV
19 May 2023